Coffee, Tea & Sweets

Adult Coloring Book
And Cookbook

Marg Ruttan

Featuring thirty coffee, tea and sweets full-sized pictures to color as well as thirty pages with smaller versions of each coloring page plus a recipe, this adult coloring book will provide you with hours of coloring fun. Relax and enjoy these designs as you choose your color palate and bring them to life.

Coloring has been proven to help us relax and relieve stress. It is my hope that this book can do that for you.

If you would like some free coloring pages and some good coloring tips, visit my website at www. coloringfunforadults.com

And to join my newsletter and receive five free coloring pages just go to www.coloringfunforadults. com/subscribe and sign up.

Happy Coloring,
Marg

Bibliographical Note:
Coffee, Tea & Sweets is a new work, first published by
Blue Jeans Publishing in 2016

International Standard Book Number
ISBN - 978-0-9950041-4-6

Recipes For You to Enjoy

Coffee and tea just seem to go with sweets and other goodies so I decided to include some recipes   that I find work really well with a warm cup of coffee or tea. These recipes are all really easy to make and are truly delicious. I guess some things never change. I have published many cookbooks over the years and so even now, when food is involved I think of recipes. I hope you enjoy this little quirk of mine and that you use the recipes over and over again.

I have created 30 coloring pages and then I've taken those pages and adapted them to include a recipe on each. Hope you enjoy this part coloring book, part cookbook! Please let me know how the recipes turn out for you. And I'd love to see some of your colored pictures as well. You can post them on my Facebook page at www.facebook.com/coloringfunforadults

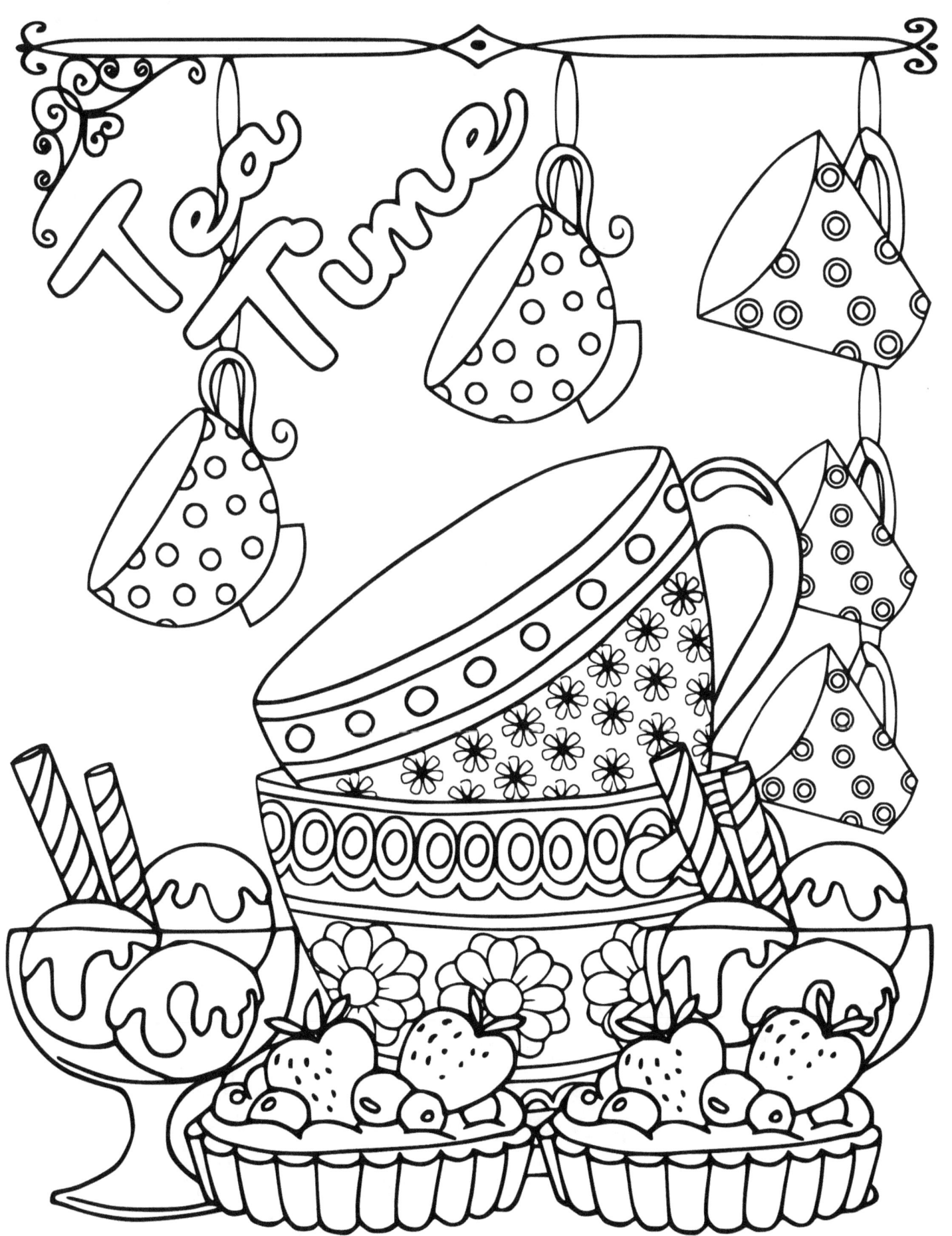

S
a
l
m
o
n

S
a
n
d
w
i
c
h
e
s

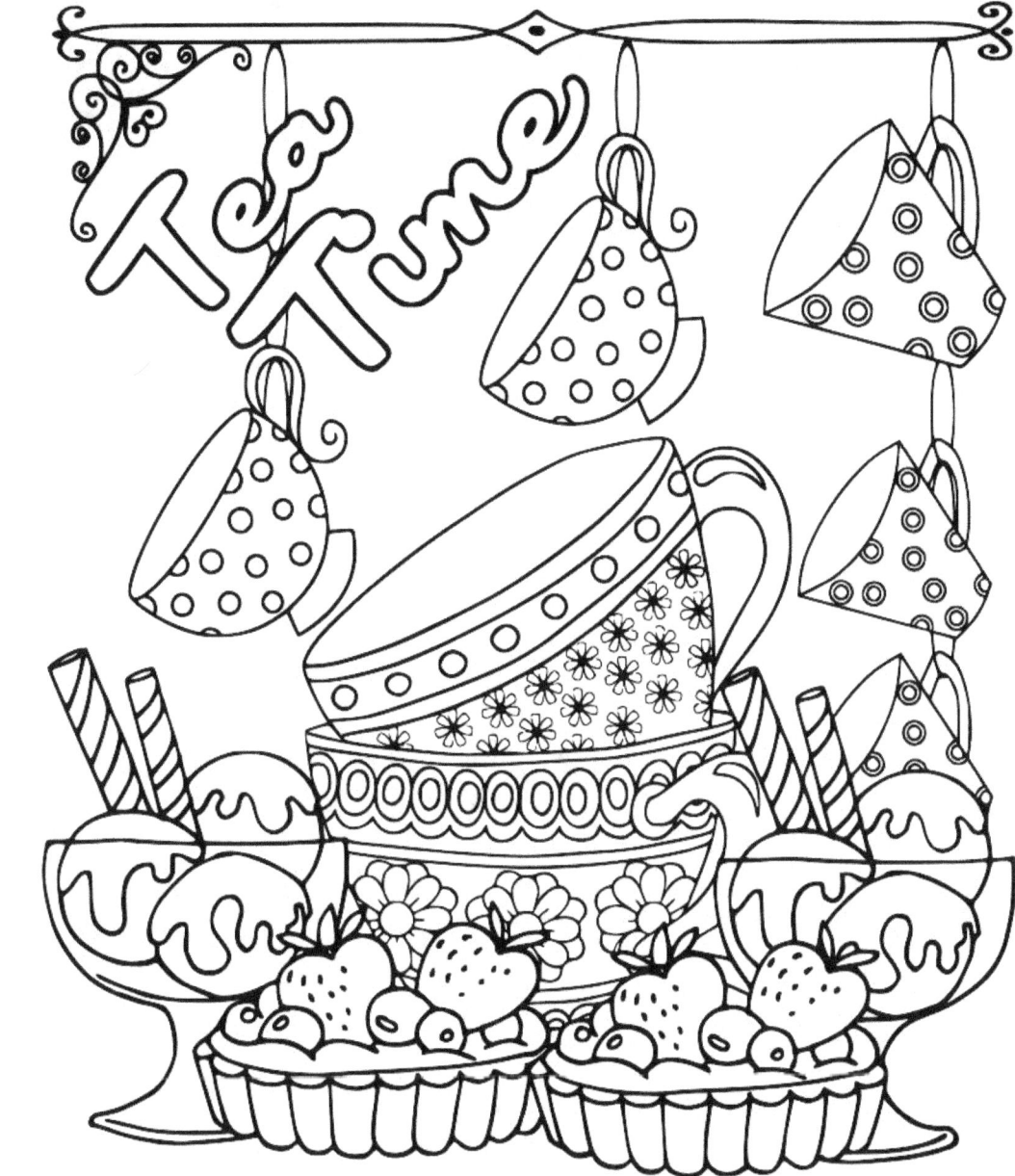

Salmon sandwiches are another British favorite to add to a tea table. Please, please, if you are making these, use fresh salmon, not the canned kind. It really doesn't make very good sandwiches and the fresh is so much better.

2 cups cooked, flaked fresh salmon
1/2 tsp. salt
1/4 tsp. pepper
1/4 cup mayonnaise
1/4 cup cream cheese
12 slices bread of your choice

When buying salmon it's best to get the skinless varitey. That way you don't have to skin it once it's cooked. To cook the salmon, place in a medium pot, cover with water and bring to a boil. Simmer for about 15 minutes. Remove from heat and drain. Cover with cold water and let stand several minues. Once the salmon is cooled, flake it with a fork in a bowl. Add the salt, pepper, and mayonnaise and stir well. Spread the cream cheese on the bread slices. Divide salmon among six slices and spread evenly over bread. Top with the remaining bread. Trim crusts and cut bread into small servings.

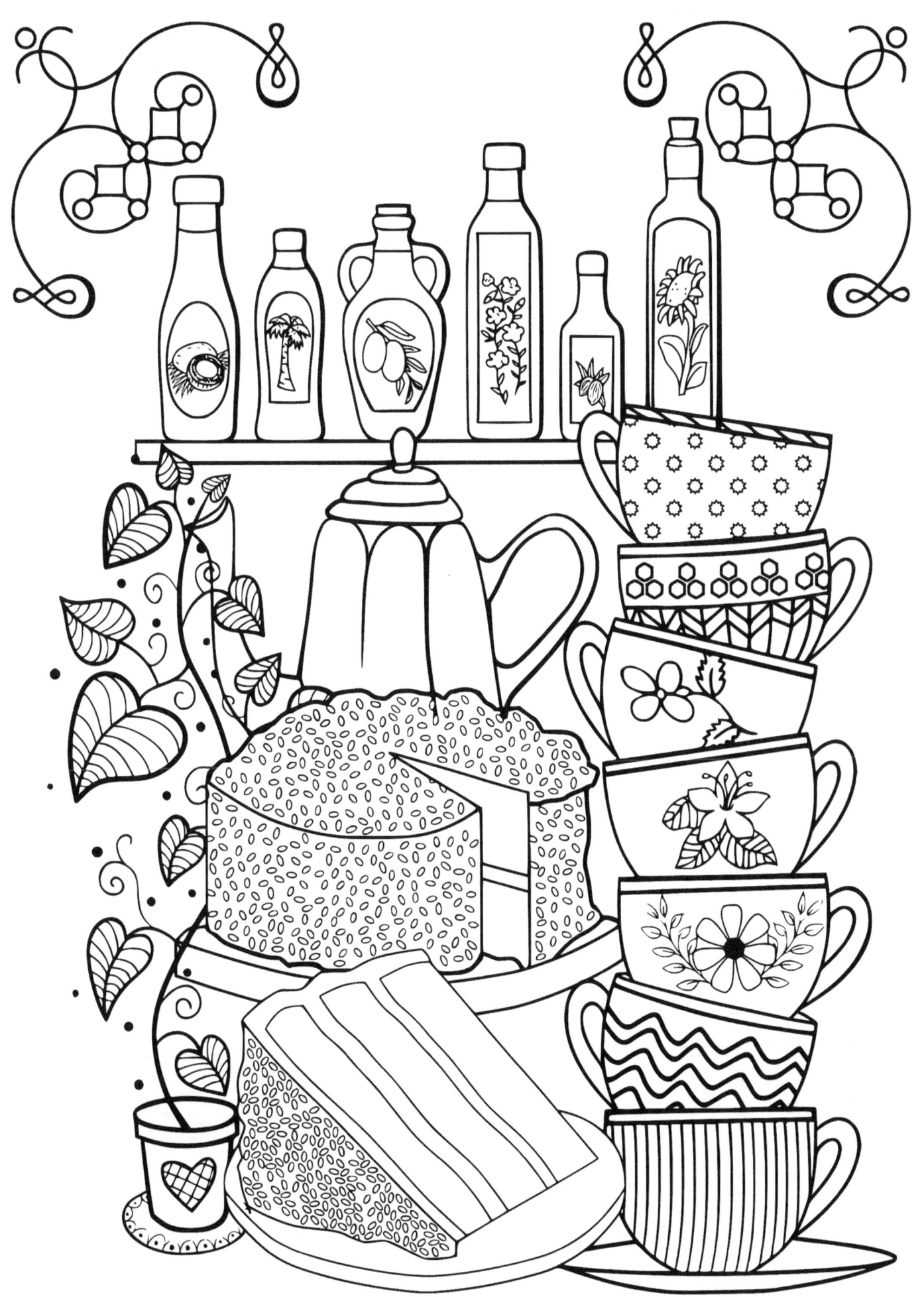

Best Ever Chocolate Cake

Chocolate cake is one of my favorite treats and I've made this recipe for years. It's simple and quick and makes a rich, moist cake every time. It's especially good with a nice cup of coffee.

1 cup granulated sugar
4 tbsp. cocoa
2 tsp. baking soda
1 tsp. salt
2 cups all-purpose flour
1 cup mayonnaise
1 cup hot water

Preheat oven to 350F. Butter a pair of layer cake pans and set aside. In a large bowl combine sugar and cocoa. Stir, removing al lumps from cocoa. Add baking soda, salt and flour. Mix thoroughly. Add mayonnaise and mix well. Pour in hot water and stir quickly, beating until the batter is smooth. Pour into pans and bake for about 25 to 35 minutes or until a toothpick inserted in the center of the cake comes out clean. Cool on racks for 10 minutes. Run a thin knife around the edge of the cake to loosen the sides from the pan. Carefully remove cake from pans. Let cool. Ice with frosting recipe below. Sprinkle with chocolate sprinkles if desired.

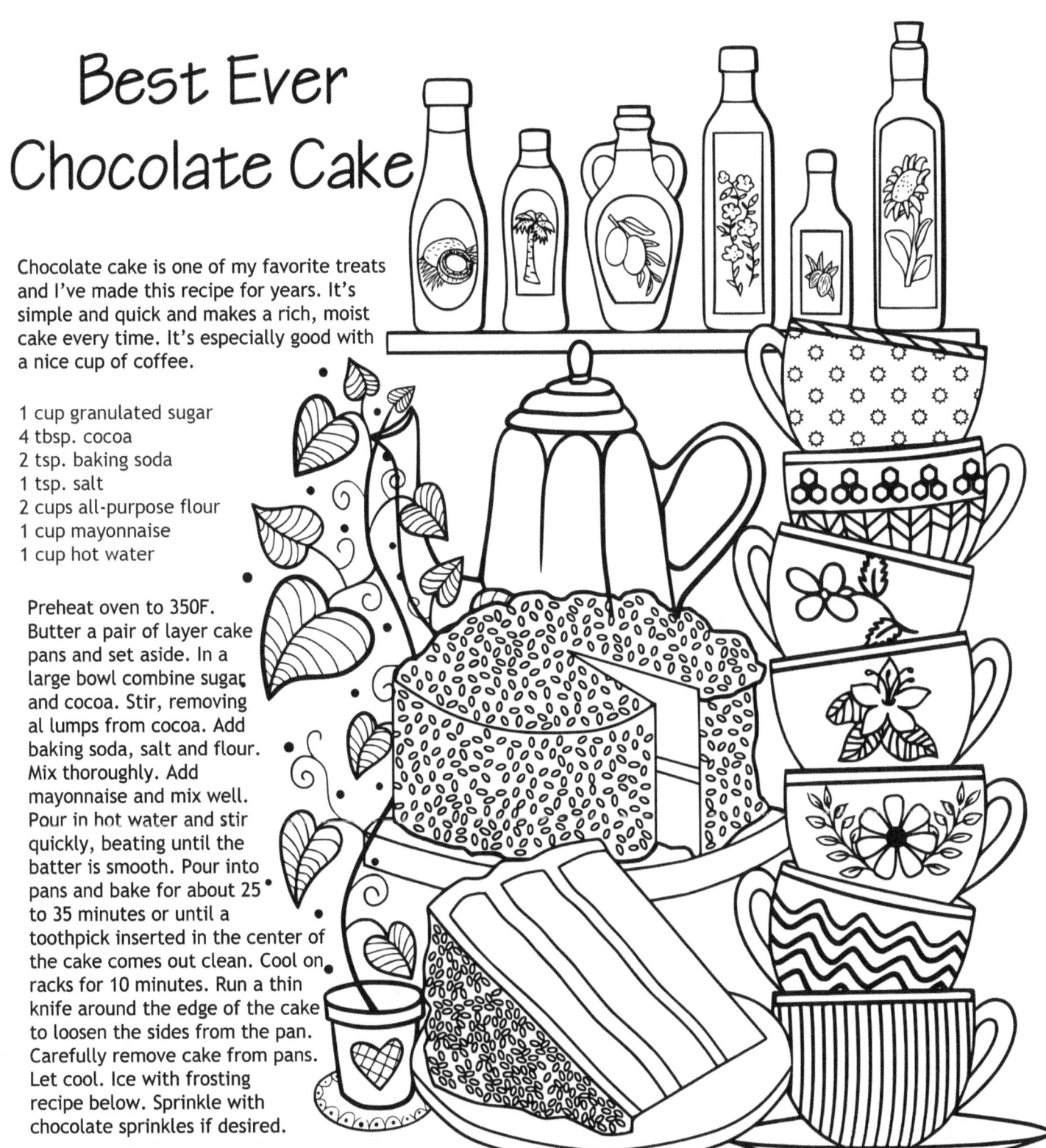

Yummy Chocolate Frosting

2 cups icing sugar
4 tbsp. cocoa
4 tbsp. melted butter
4 tbsp. milk

Combine icing sugar and cocoa, removing all lumps from cocoa. Mix in butter and milk, beating until smooth and creamy. Ice cake using generous amounts of the frosting.

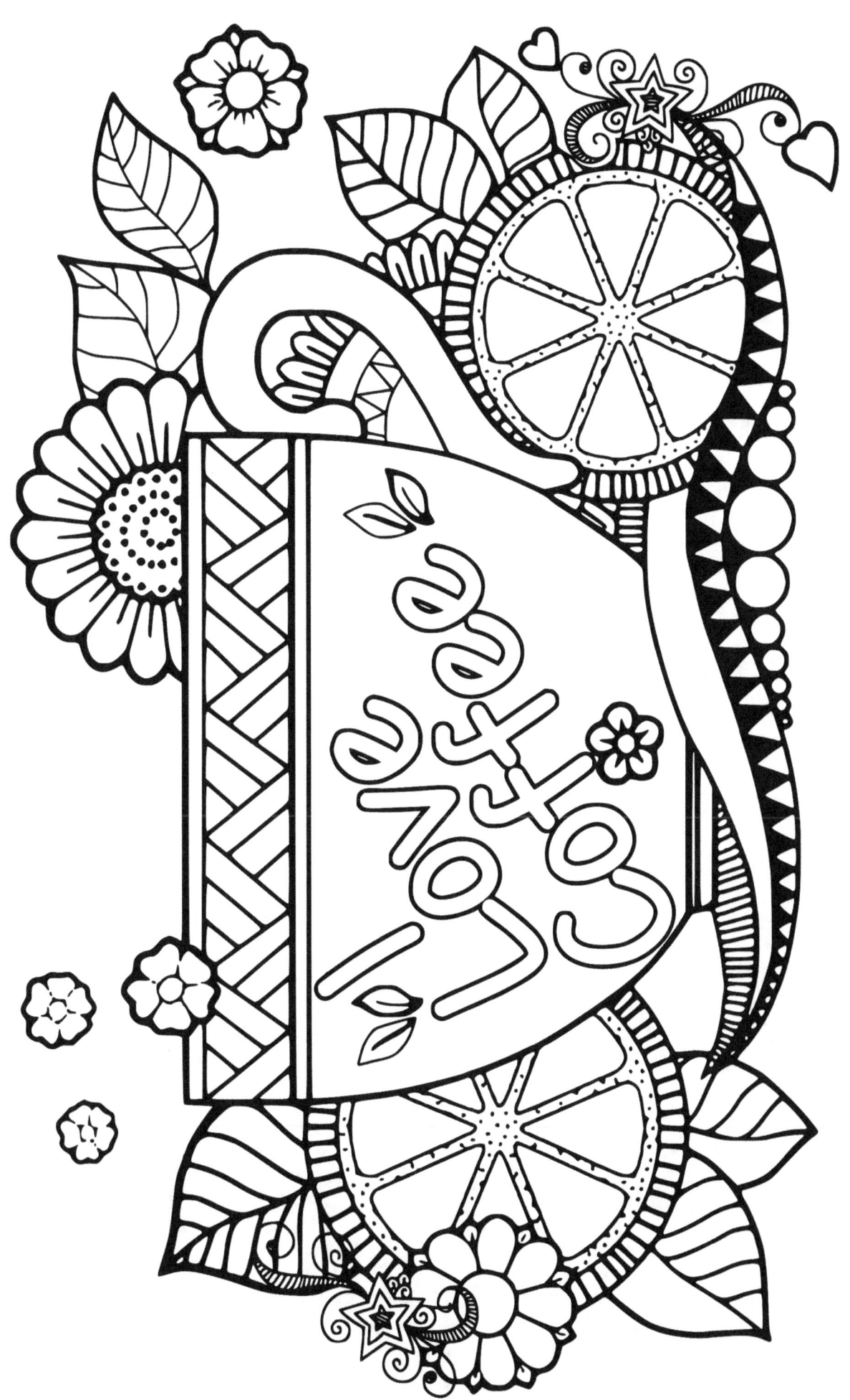

Crunchy Lemon Cookies

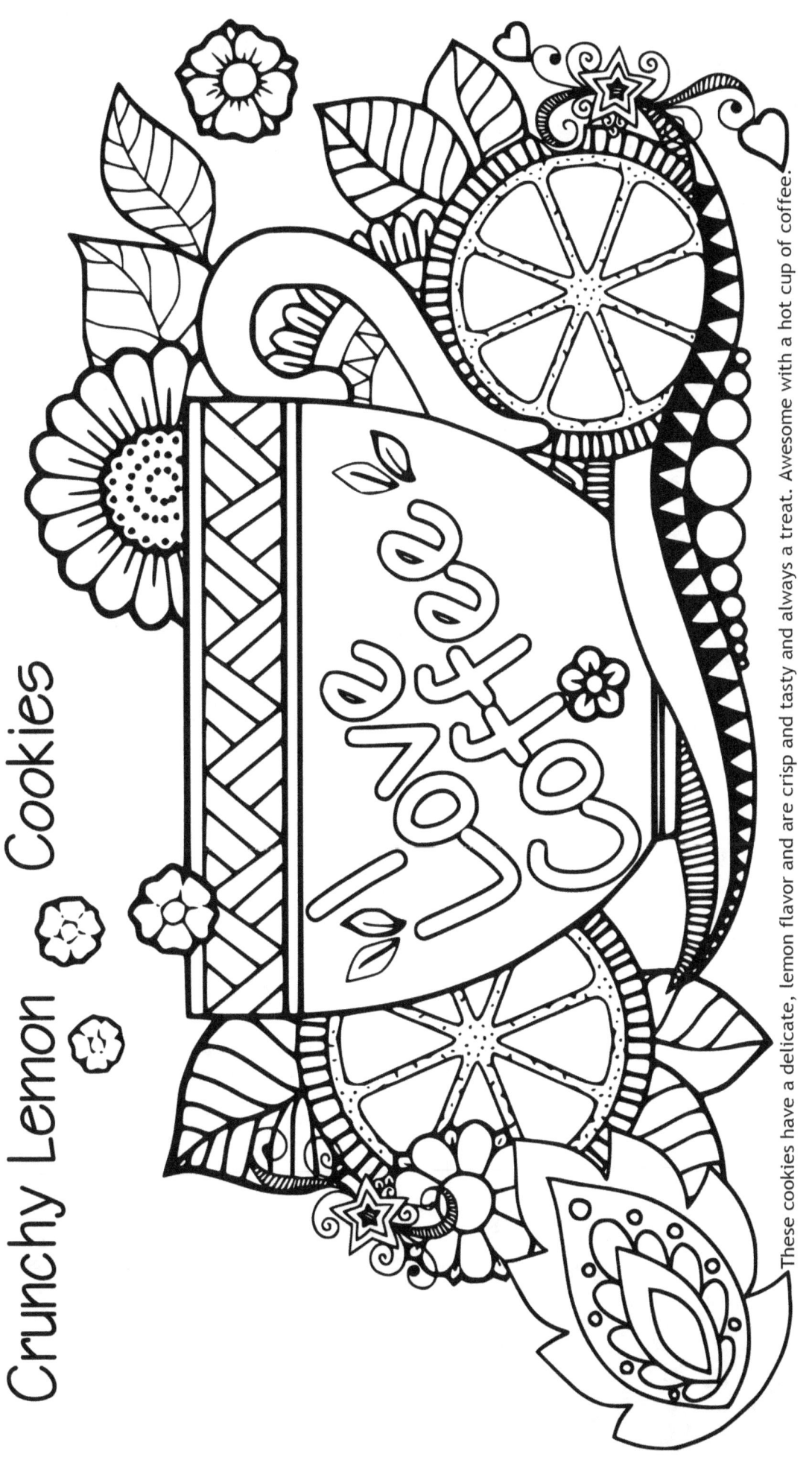

These cookies have a delicate, lemon flavor and are crisp and tasty and always a treat. Awesome with a hot cup of coffee.

Preheat oven to 375F. In a large bowl cream butter and sugars together. Add egg and beat thoroughly. Stir in lemon rind, lemon juice, baking soda, baking powder and salt. Gradually mix in flour. Form dough into 1" balls and place on ungreased cookie sheets. With the tines of a fork that has been dipped in flour, gently press balls into 1 1/2" circles. Sprinkle each circle with a bit of granulated sugar. Bake for 7 to 8 minutes or until golden brown.

3/4 cup butter
1/4 cup granulated sugar
1/2 cup packed brown sugar
1 egg
2 tbsp. grated lemon rind
2 tbsp. lemon juice
1/2 tsp. baking soda
1/2 tsp. baking powder
1/2 tsp. salt
2 cups all-purpose flour

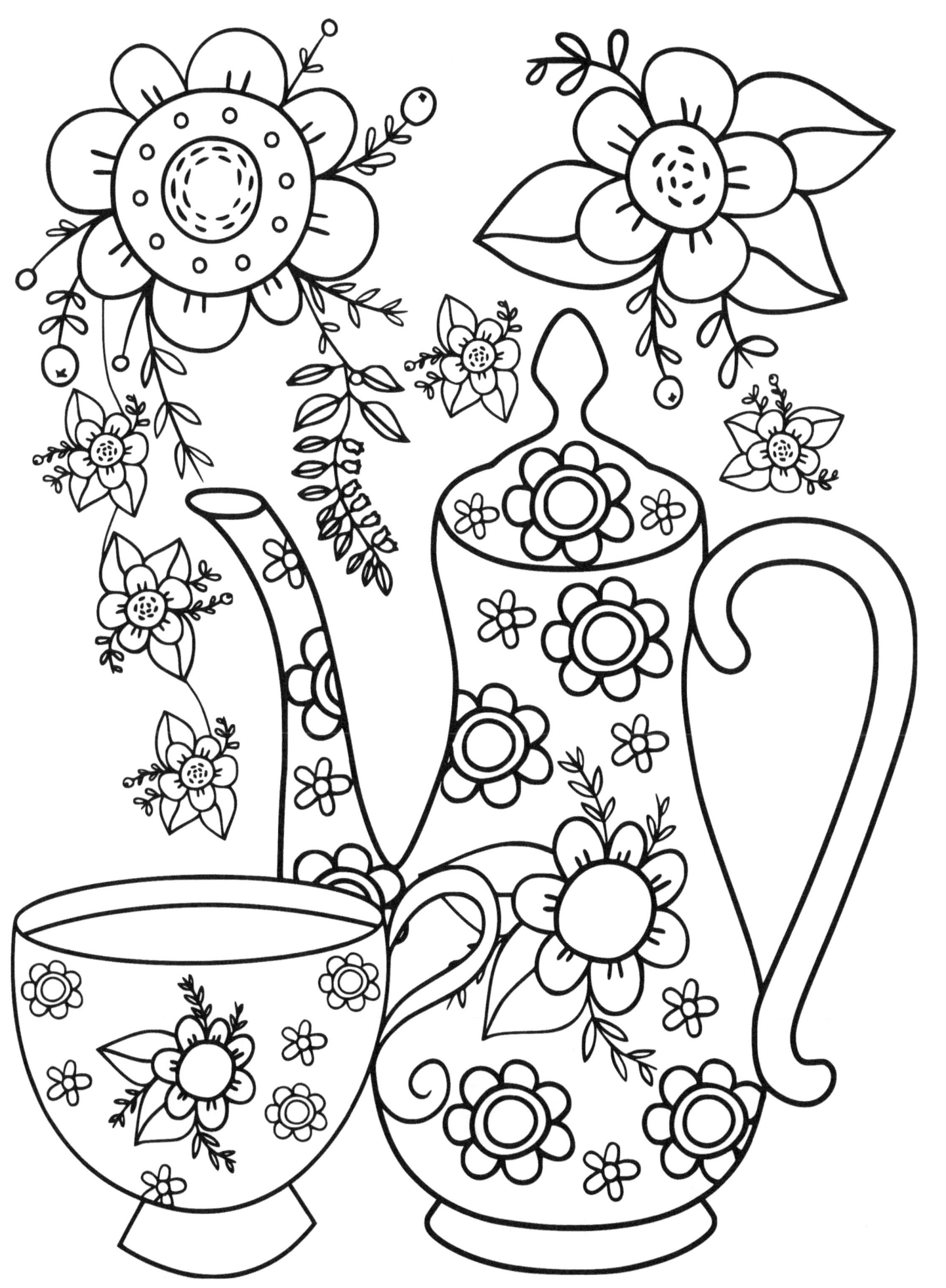

Seafood Mushrooms

Anyone who loves seafood will want these served often. They are great for afternoon tea and have such a lovely flavor. Just make them up and watch them disappear.

4 oz. cream cheese, softened
1/2 cup butter
1 tsp. horseradish
1 tsp. garlic powder
4 oz. shrimp, rinsed and cut into tiny pieces
4 3/4 oz. crab, membrane removed
24 large mushrooms, stems removed

Preheat oven to 350F. Mix together cheese, butter, horseradish and garlic powder. Beat until light and smooth. Add shrimp and crab and beat together well. Stuf mushrooms with mixture. Place on baking sheet. Bake for about 15 minutes or until filling begins to get a bit crusty. Serve while still warm.

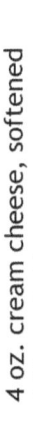

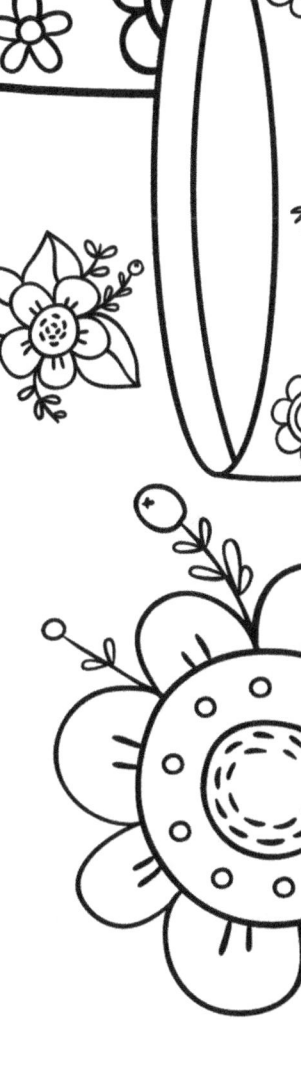

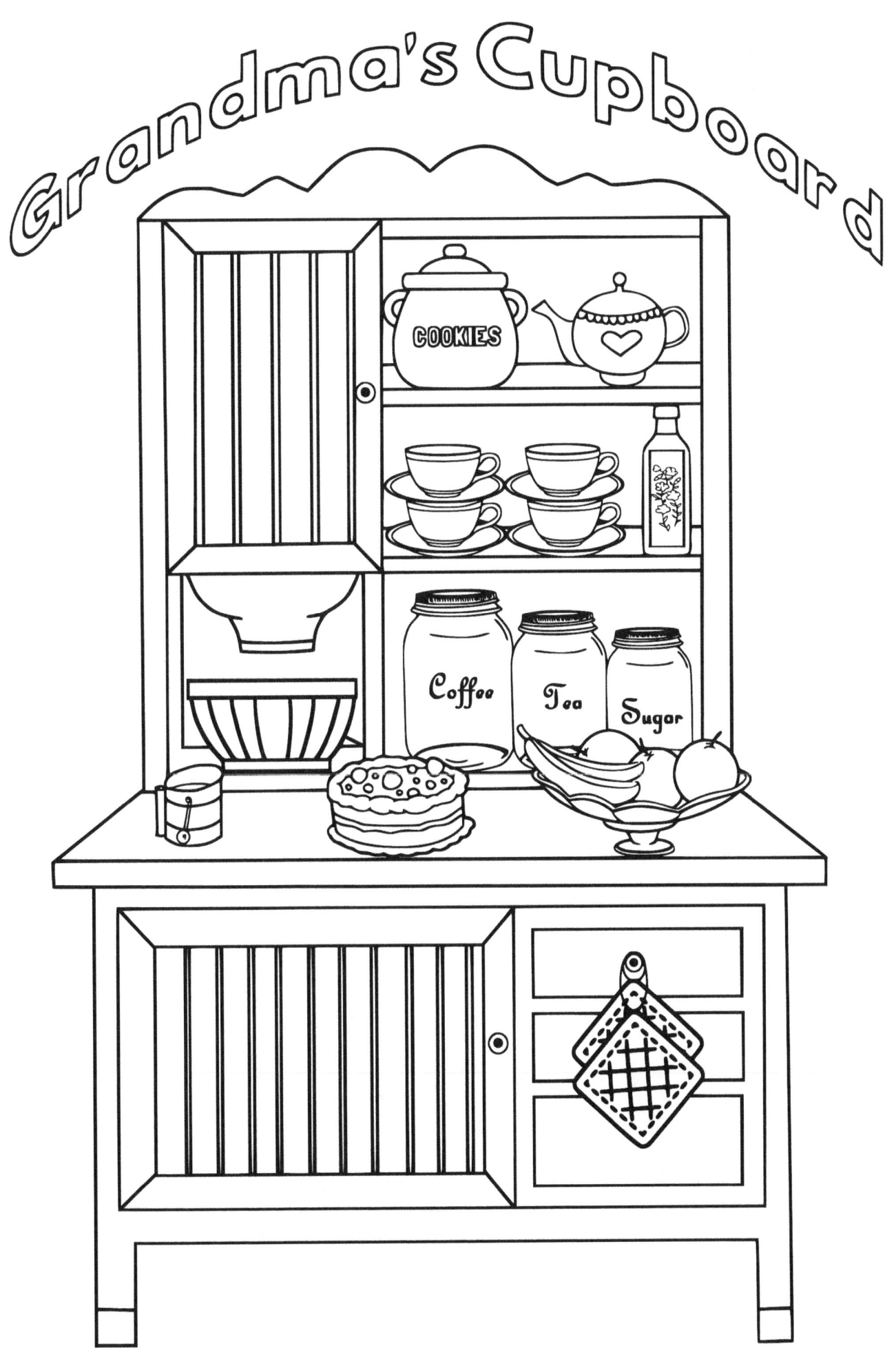

Orange Pecan Crisps

Here's another cookie that has wonderful flavor. Easy to make and they sure disappear in a hurry!

3/4 cup butter
1 egg
2 tbsp. orange juice
1 1/2 tsp. baking powder
2 cups all-purpose flour

3/4 cup granulated sugar
2 tbsp. grated orange rind
1/2 tsp. baking soda
1/2 tsp. salt
3/4 cup finely chopped pecans

Preheat oven to 375F. In a large bowl, cream butter and sugar together. Add egg and beat well. Stir in orange rind, orange juice, baking soda, baking powder and salt. Mix well. Gradually mix in flour. Fold in chopped pecans. Form dough into 1" balls and place on ungreased cookie sheets. Using the tines of a fork which has been dipped in flour, gently press into 1 1/2" circles. Bake for 8 - 10 minutes.

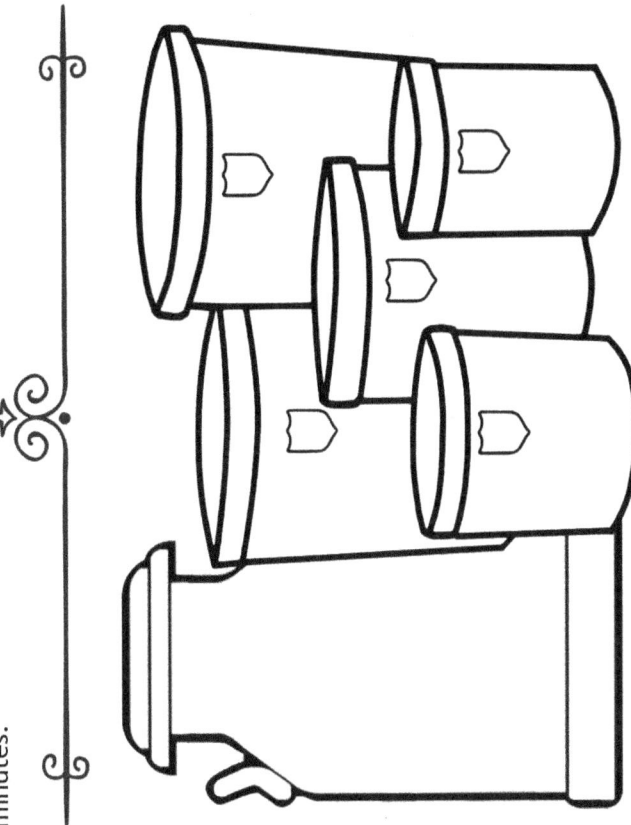

GRANDMAS PANTRY

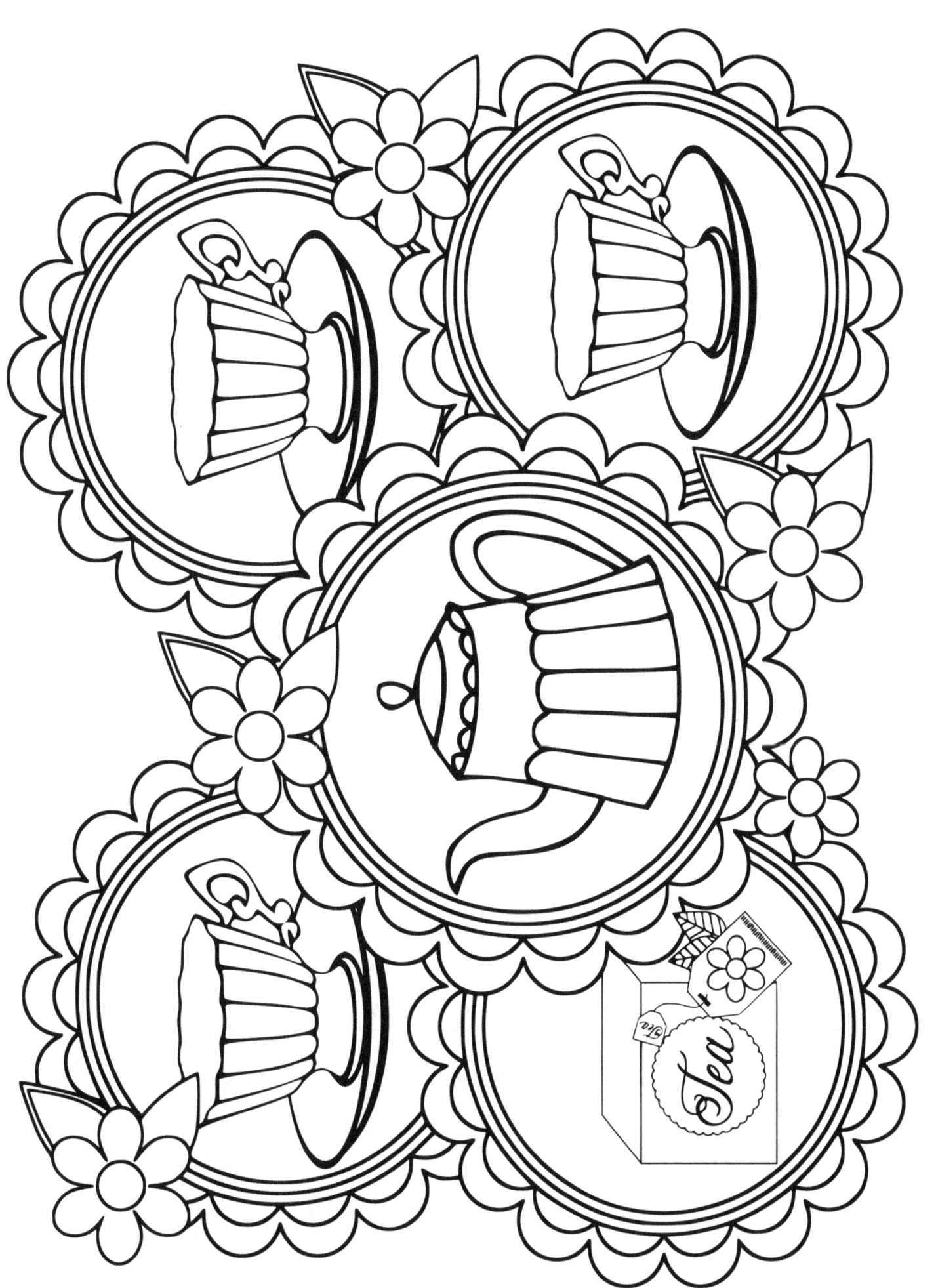

English Scones

The British often serve scones with tea. And they also often serve jam. These scones are easy to make and are delicious. They are very soft and because they are made with butter they have a wonderful, rich taste.

2 cups all-purpose flour
2 tbsp. granulated sugar
1 tsp. salt
4 tsp. baking powder
1/2 cup butter
1 cup cold milk

Preheat oven to 425 F. Mix **all** dry ingredients together in a bowl. Blend thoroughly. Cut in butter until the mixture is crumbly. Pour in milk. Stir to combine. Dough will be very soft. Turn out on a lightly floured surface. Sprinkle with about 2 tbsp. flour. Gently knead and work this flour into the dough. Pat dough to 3/4" thickness. Cut scones out with a small round cookie cutter. Place on an ungreased baking sheet. Bake for 12 - 15 mihutes or until tops are golden brown.

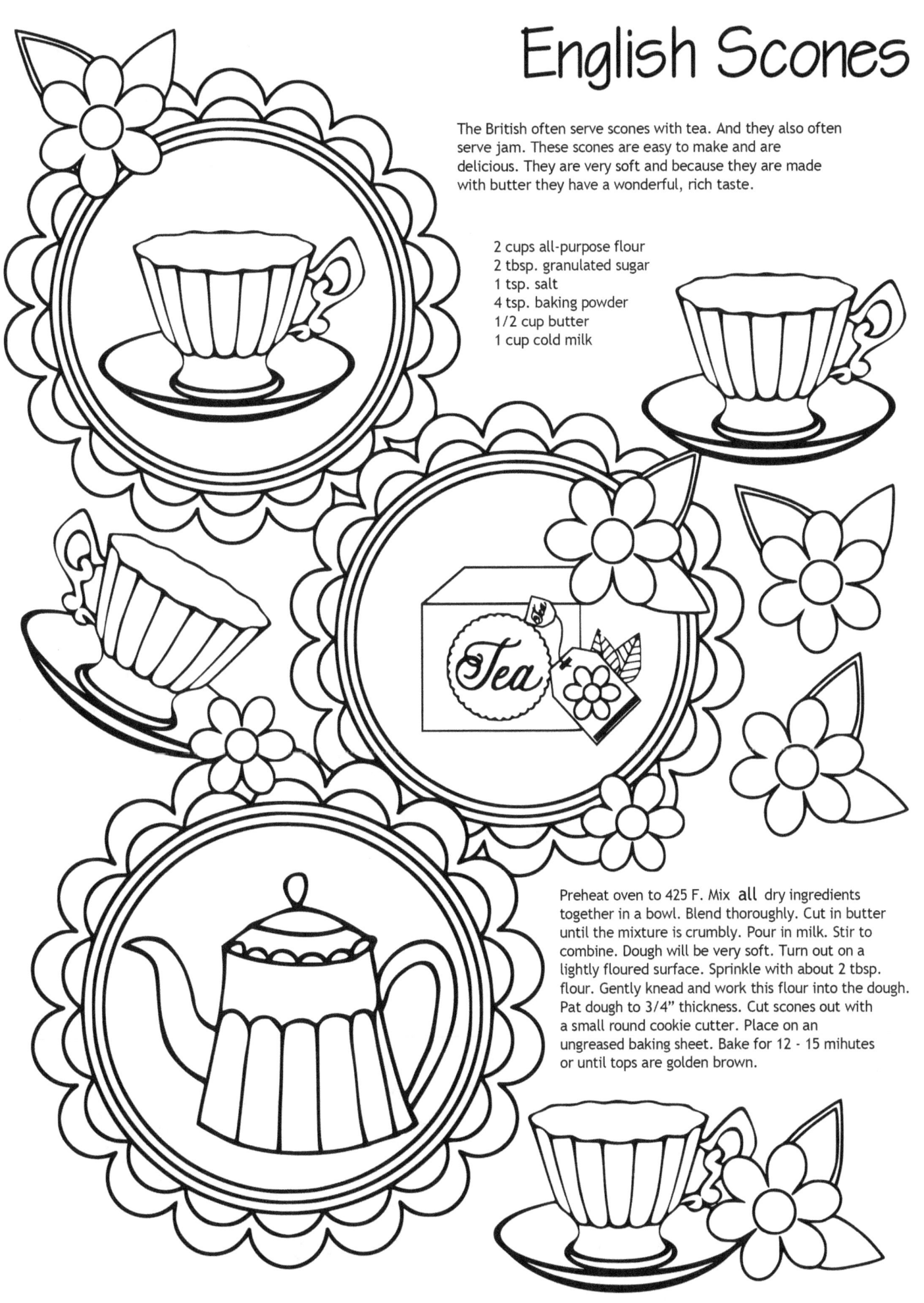

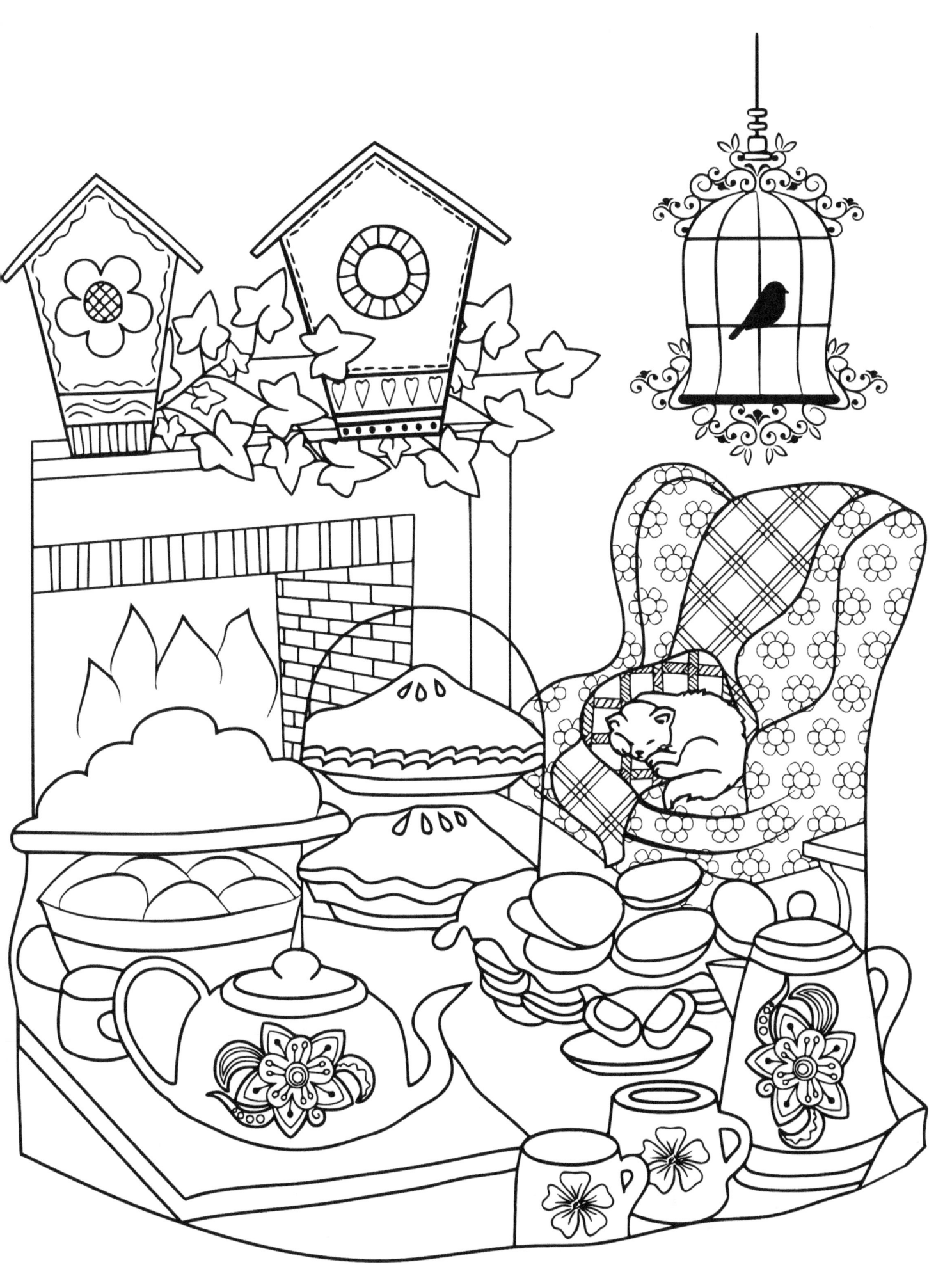

Tuna Pinwheels

These are easy to make and are so well liked. They are colorful and have a delightful flavor.

1 cup whipped cream cheese
1 tbsp. lemon juice
2 cans tuna, packed in water
1/2 tsp. salt
4 - 7" soft tacos

1/4 red onion, finely chopped
1 tsp. dried dill
2 medium sized tomatoes, seeded and diced
1/4 tsp. pepper

Combine all ingredients except tacos. Spread mixture evenly over tacos and tightly roll them up. Cut off ends. Wrap in wax paper and refrigerate until ready to serve. Cut each taco into 8 slices and serve as soon as they are cut.

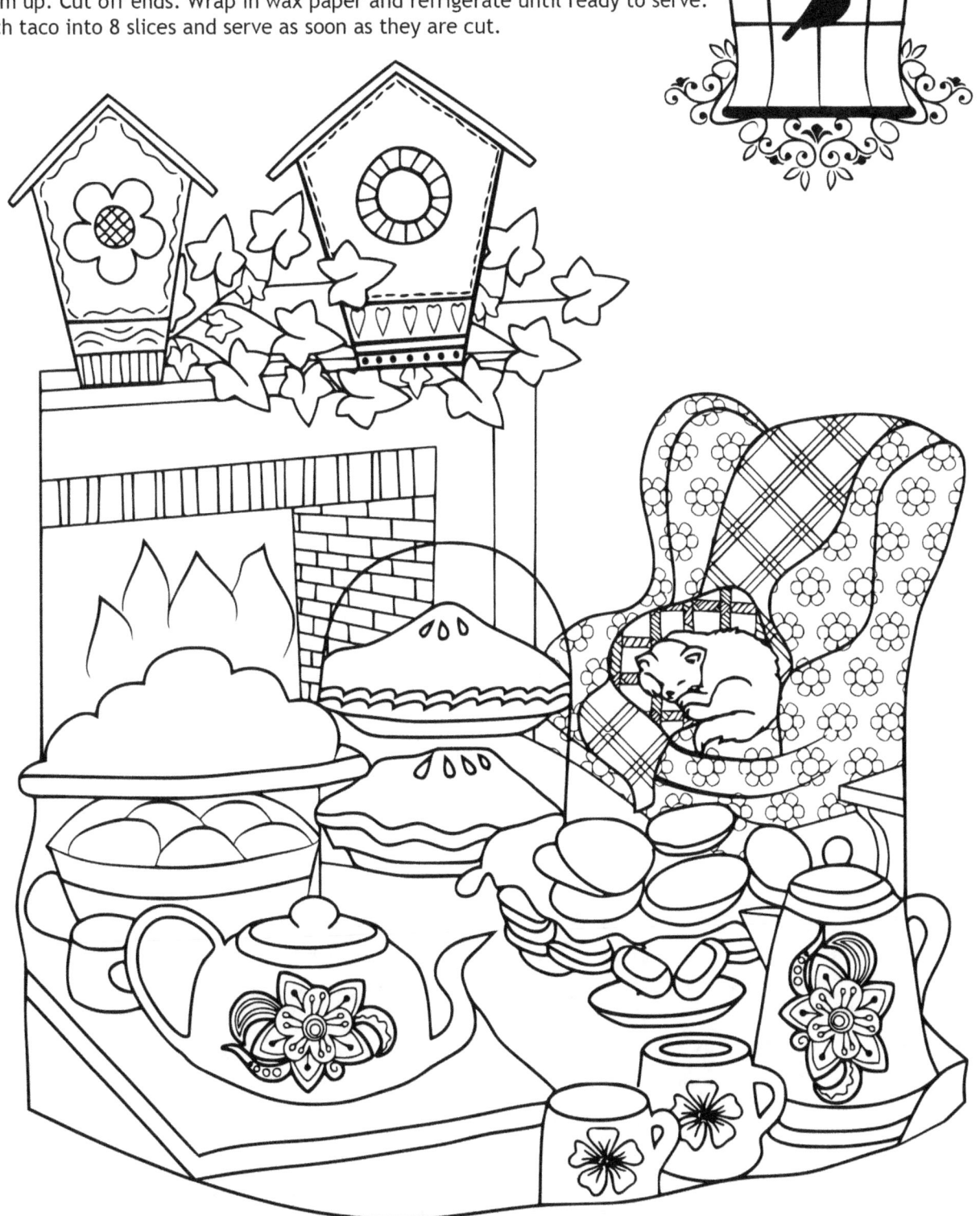

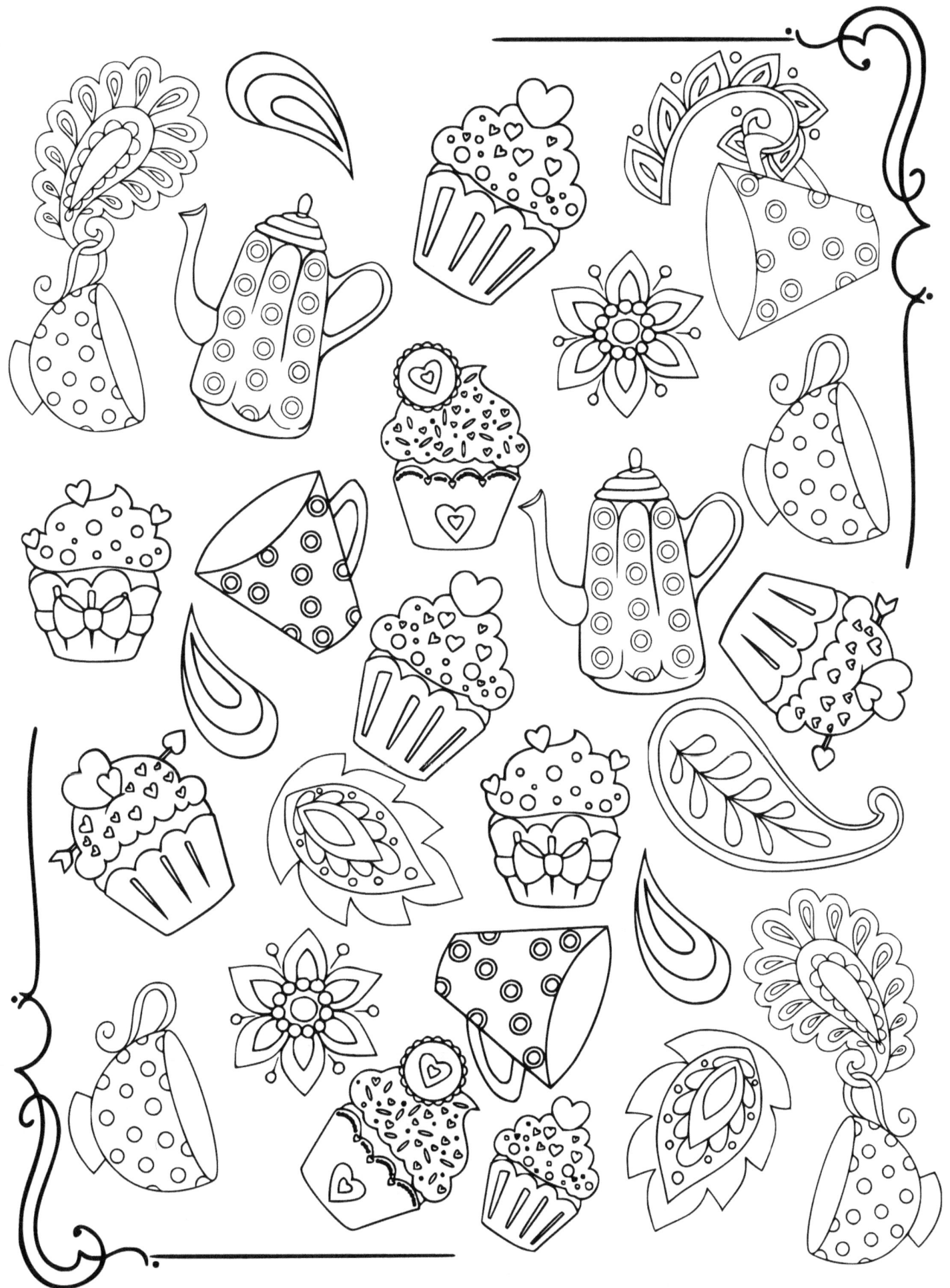

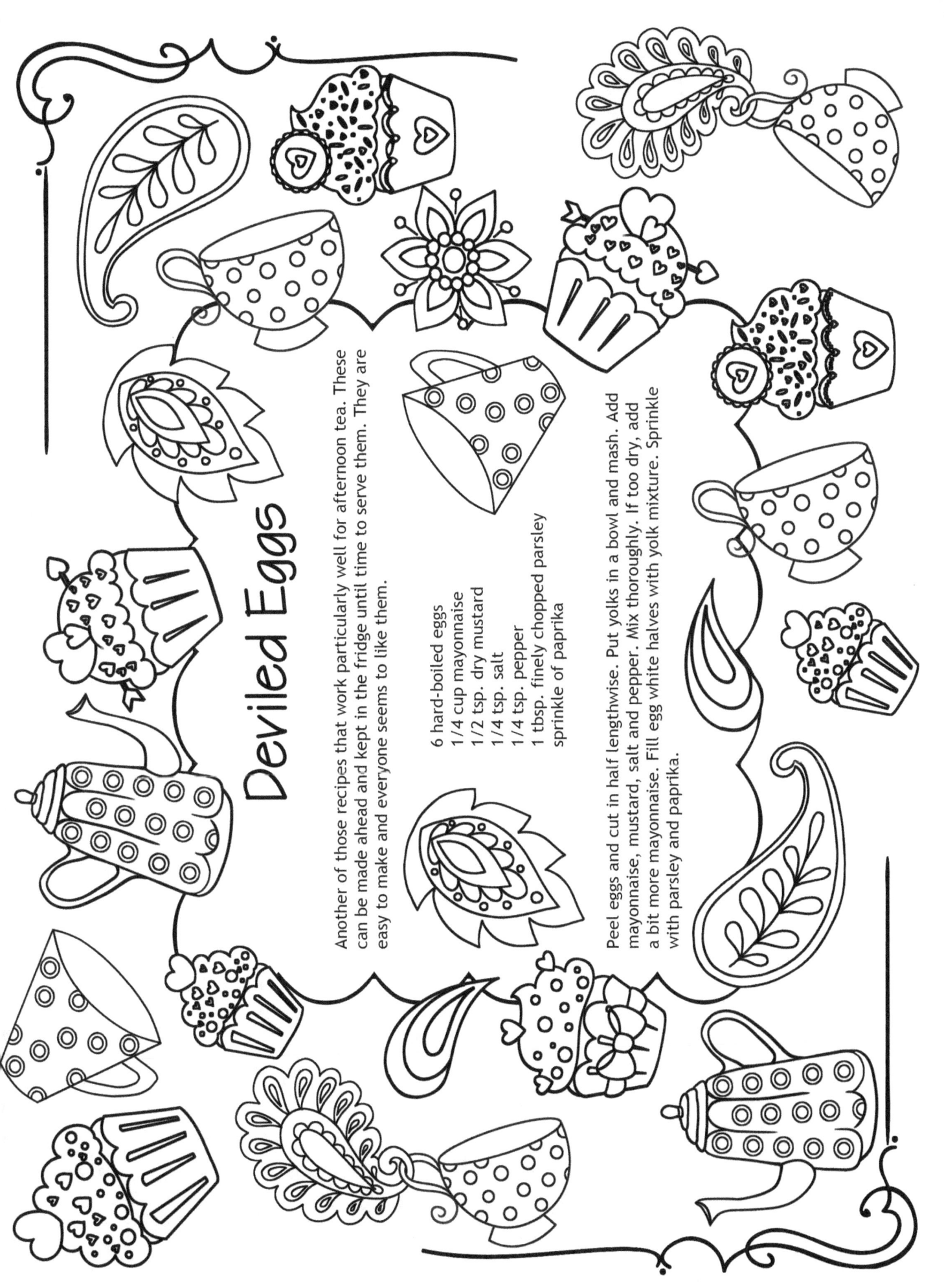

Deviled Eggs

Another of those recipes that work particularly well for afternoon tea. These can be made ahead and kept in the fridge until time to serve them. They are easy to make and everyone seems to like them.

6 hard-boiled eggs
1/4 cup mayonnaise
1/2 tsp. dry mustard
1/4 tsp. salt
1/4 tsp. pepper
1 tbsp. finely chopped parsley
sprinkle of paprika

Peel eggs and cut in half lengthwise. Put yolks in a bowl and mash. Add mayonnaise, mustard, salt and pepper. Mix thoroughly. If too dry, add a bit more mayonnaise. Fill egg white halves with yolk mixture. Sprinkle with parsley and paprika.

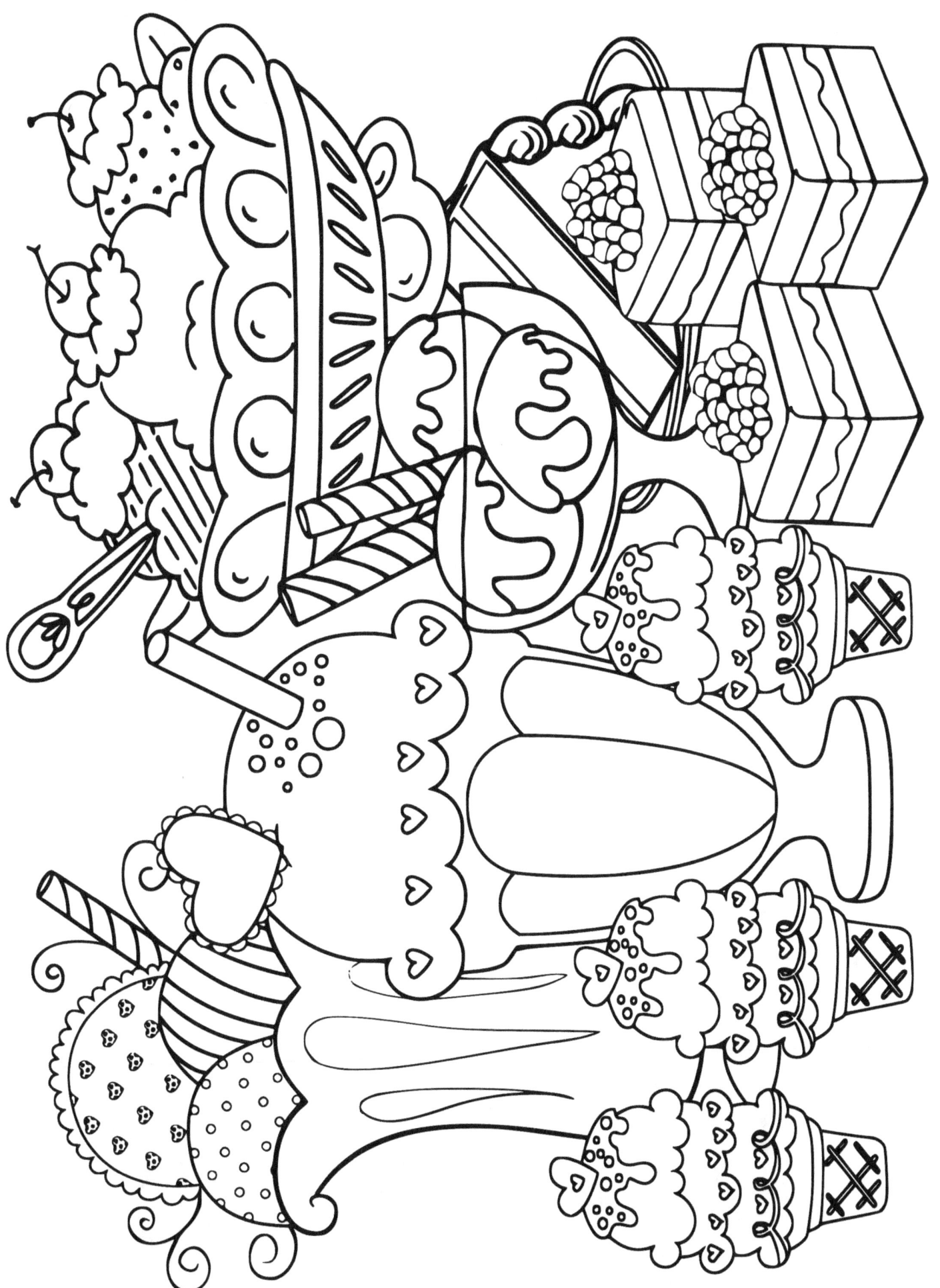

Best Ever Shortbread

Here's another recipe that is well-loved in the British Isles. I've made literally thousands of these little gems over the years and they always turn out perfectly every time. Don't limit yourself to Christmas for shortbread, have them often. And try them with your favolrite ice cream...they're yummy.

1 1/2 cups butter
2 1/2 cups all-purpose flour
3/4 cup icing sugar

Preheat oven to 350F. In a large bowl cream butter and icing sugar. Gradually mix in flour. Force dough through a cookie press on ungreased cookie sheets. Bake 6 - 7 minutes or until golden brown.

Variations:
Lemon Shortbread: Add 1 tbsp. finely grated lemon rind and 1 tsp. lemon juice to butter mixture.
Almond Shortbread: Add 1 tsp. almond extract to butter mixture. Place a piece of slivered almond on top of each cookie.

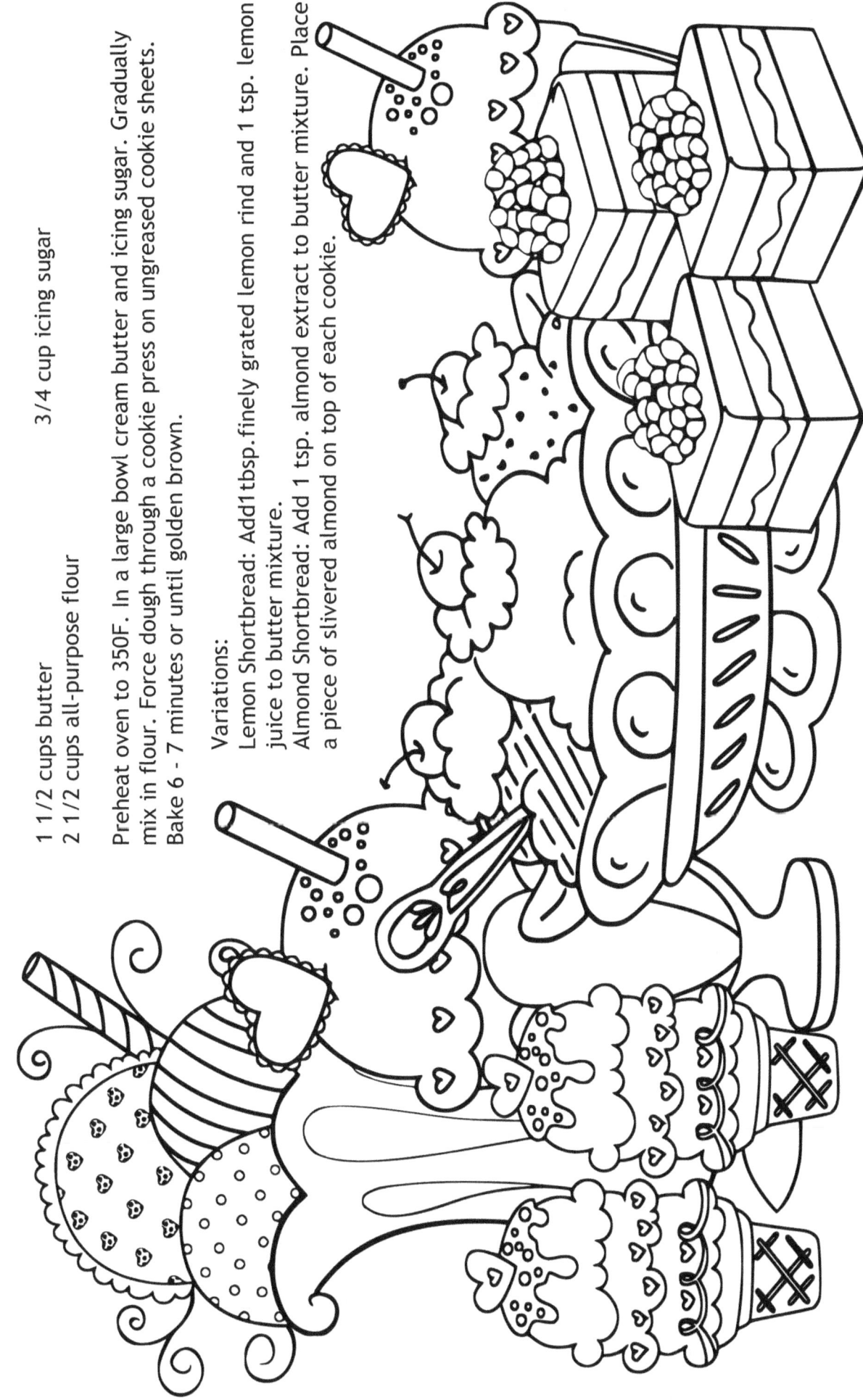

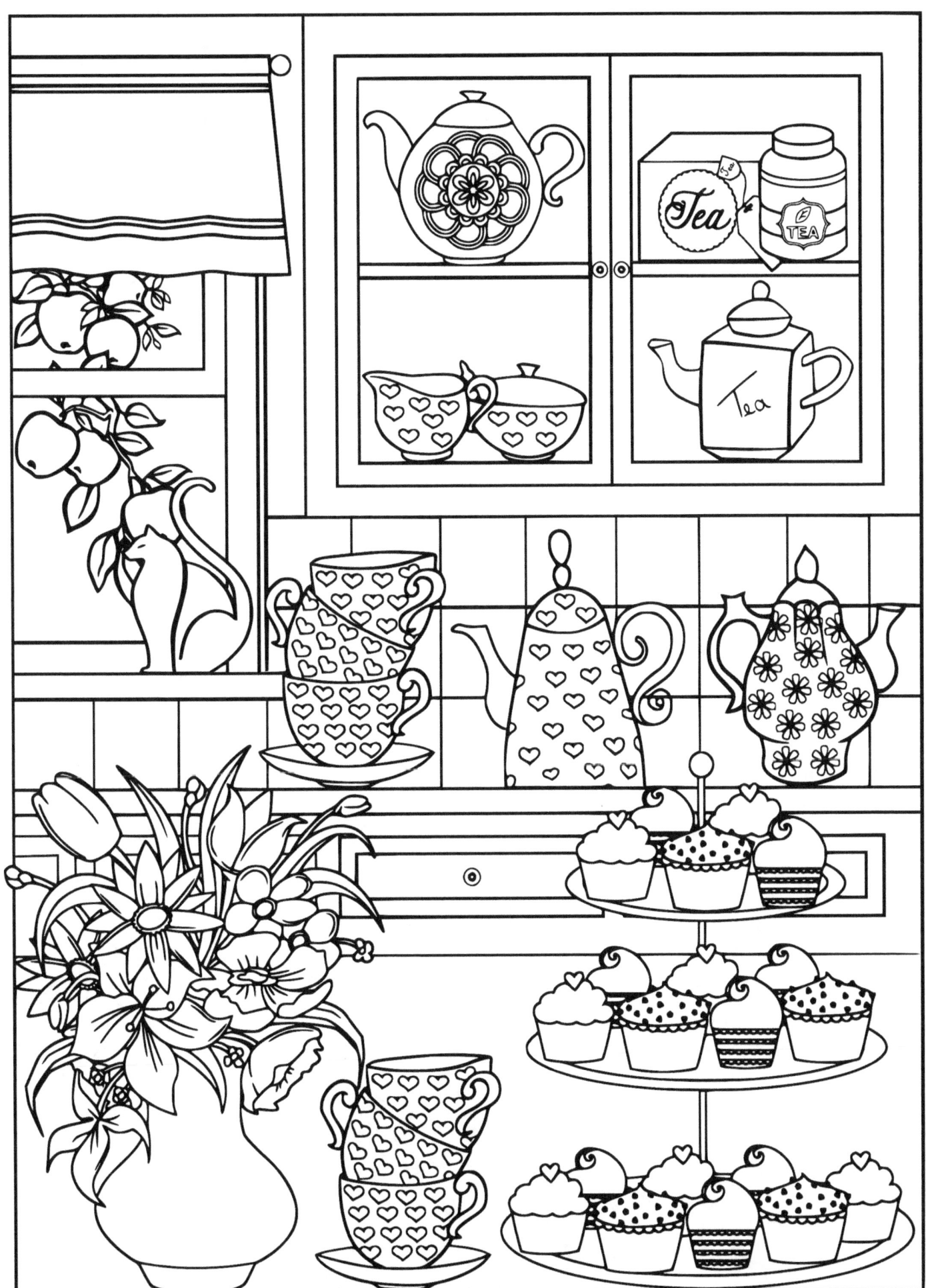

Salmon Remingtons

When I was growing up my Mom always talked about Grandma making salmon remingtons and how good they were. Unfortunately, Mom didn't have a recipe but I finally convinced her to figure out how they were made. I'm glad I nagged her as these are a really delicious treat. And they'd be perfect for afternoon tea too.

12 large tart shells, baked
1 tbsp. butter
2 celery stalks, finely diced
1 medium onion, finely chopped
2 tbsp. all-purpose flour
1 1/3 cups milk
4 tbsp. chopped fresh parsley
1/2 tsp. salt
1/4 tsp. white pepper
1/2 tsp. dry mustard
2 cups cooked, flaked fresh, not canned, salmon
Chopped green onion
Paprika

Preheat oven to 350F. Place baked tart shells in muffin tins. In a frying pan, over medium heat, melt butter and sauté celery and onions for about 6 - 7 minutes. Add flour and stir constantly. Cook for a minute. Gradually add milk, stirring constantly. The milk will gradually thicken to form a sauce. Add the seasonings and mustard. Cook for 5 minutes stirring constantly. Add the salmon and blend gently. Spoon the filling into the tart shells. Sprinkle with chopped green onion and paprika. Bake for about 20 minutes or until they are piping hot. Serve hot.

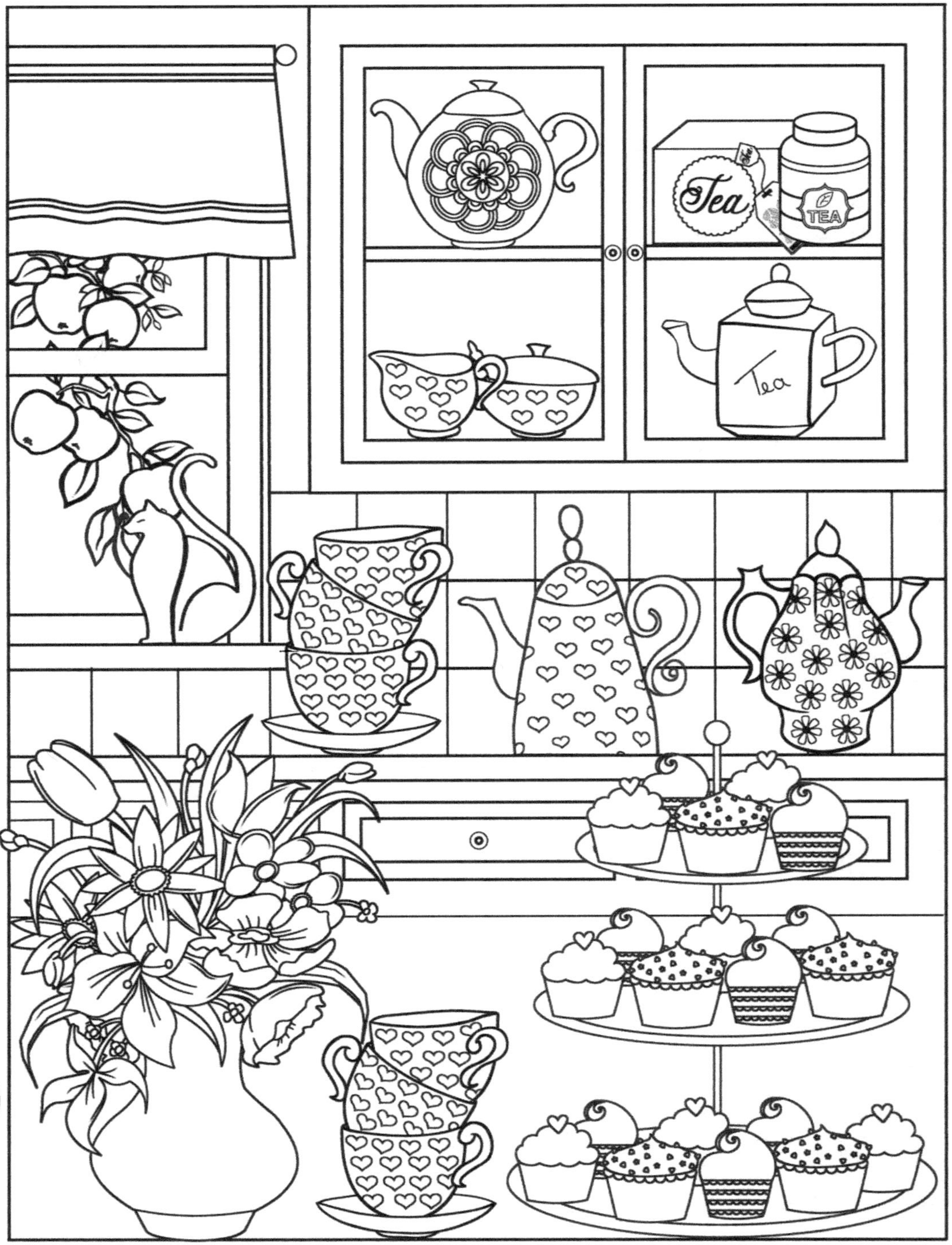

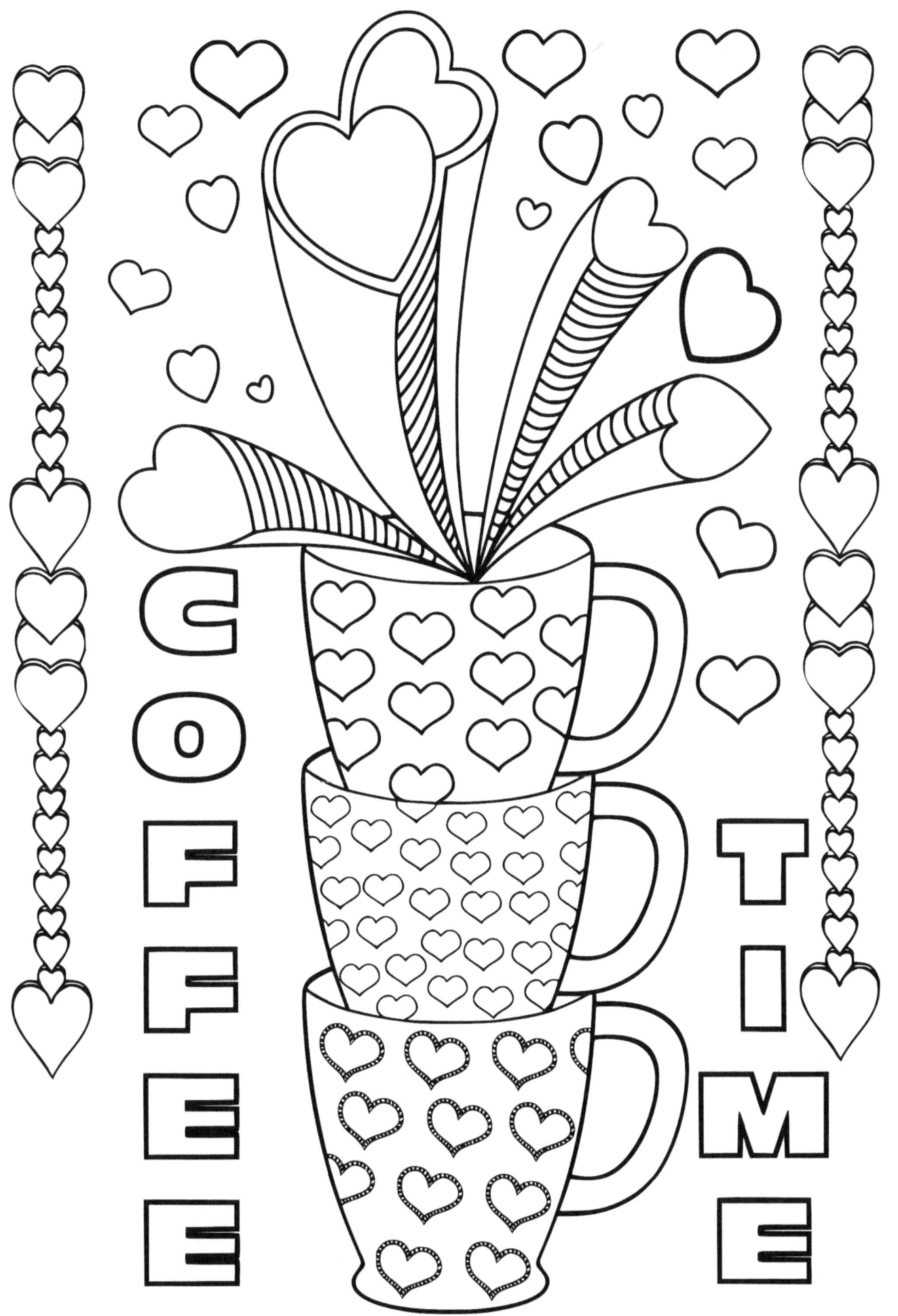

Fruited Coffee Cake

This coffee cake takes a while to bake but it's well worth the wait. A great snack with a piping hot cup of coffee.

2 tbsp. raisins
1/2 cup chopped cranberries
1 tbsp. orange juice
3/4 cup granulated sugar
1/2 tsp. baking powder
1/4 tsp. nutmeg
1 beaten egg

2/3 cup pineapple jam
1/2 tsp. grated orange rind
2 1/4 cups all-purpose flour
3/4 cup butter or margarine
1/2 tsp. baking soda
1/4 tsp. salt
3/4 cup sour milk*

*To make sour milk add 1 tsp. vinegar to milk.

Preheat oven to 350F. Grease a 10" round cake pan with a removeable bottom. Set aside. Place raisins in a small bowl. Pour enough boiling water over them to cover. Let stand 5 minutes. Drain thoroughly. Stir in jam, cranberries, orange peel and orange juice. Set aside. Stir flour and sugar together in a large mixing bowl. Using a pastry blender, cut in butter till mixture resembles coarse crumbs. Set aside 1/2 cup for crumb topping. Stir baking powder, baking soda, nutmeg and salt into remaining flour mixture. Mix well. Make a well in the center. Combine egg and milk in a small bowl. Add to flour mixture. Stir just till moistened. Spread 2/3 of the batter in the cake pan. Carefully spread the fruit filling over the batter. Spoon remaining batter in small mounds over the filling. Sprinkle with reserved crumb mixture. Bake for about 1 hour or until a toothpick inserted in the middle of the cake comes out clean. Cook in the pan on a rack for 15 minutes. Remove from pan. Top with Orange Drizzle.

Orange Drizzle: Stir together 1/2 cup icing sugar, 1/2 tsp. finely shredded orange peel and enough orange juice (1 to 2 tsp.) to make a thin icing. Drizzle over top of cake.

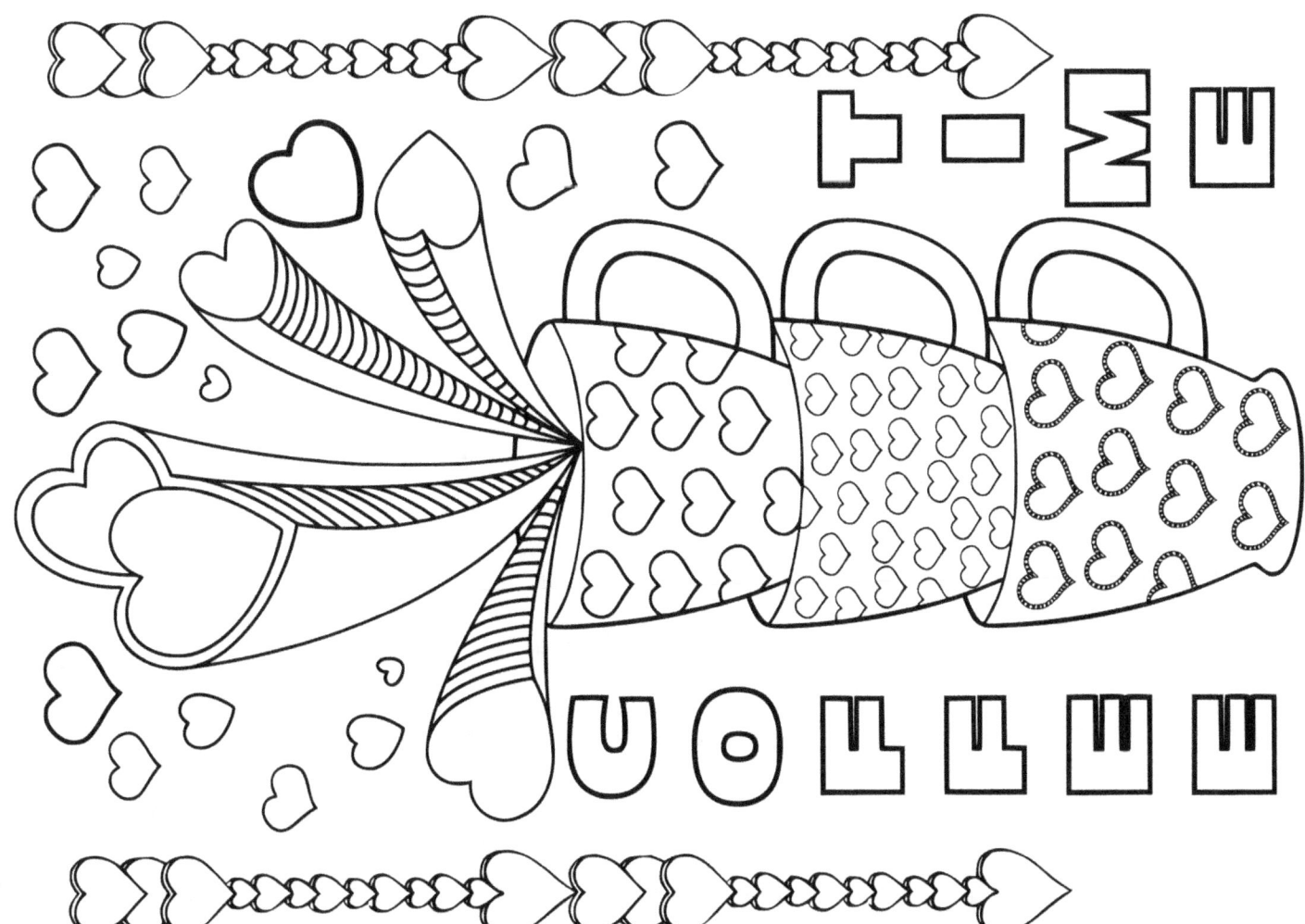

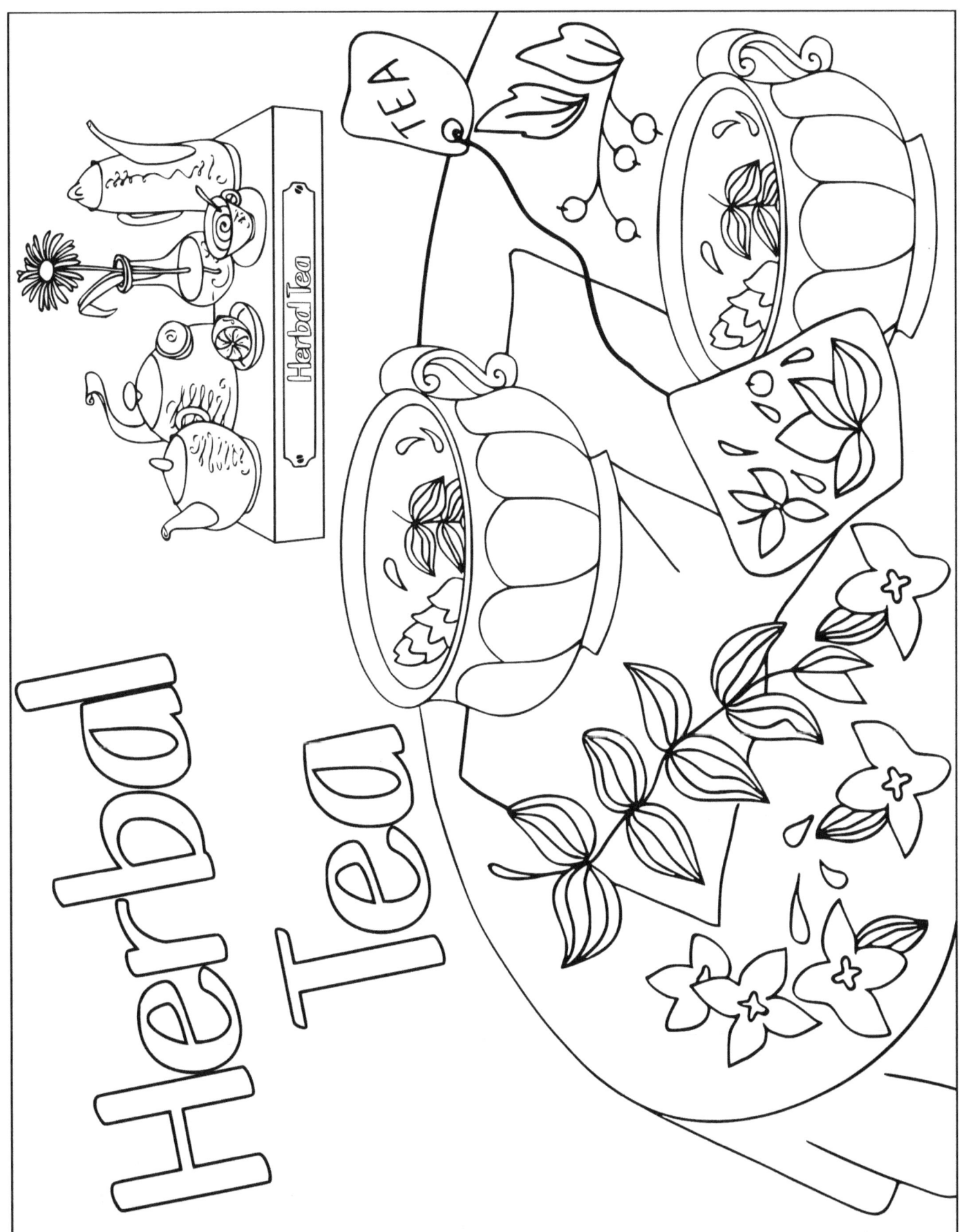

Pumpkin Tea Bread

For a full-bodied flavor this bread can't be beat. It has a deep, rich flavor and is really delicious.

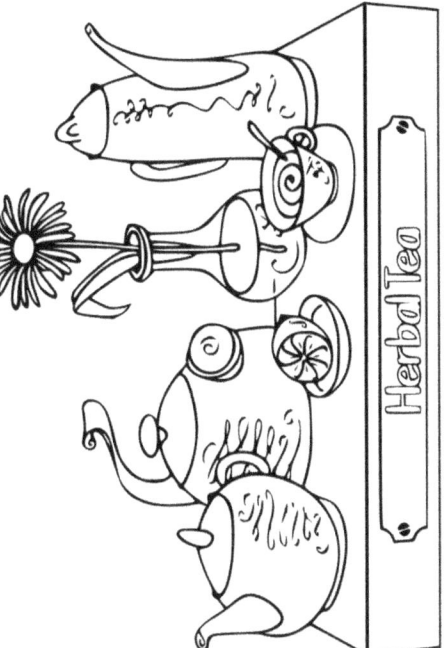

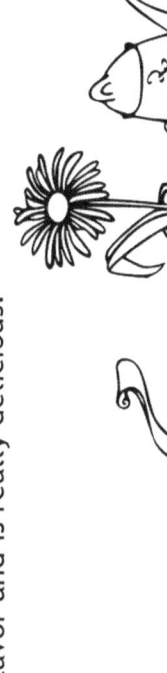

Herbal Tea

1/2 cup butter or margarine
2 eggs
1 tbsp. grated orange rind
2 1/4 cups all-purpose flour
2 tsp. baking soda
1/2 tsp. cinnamon
1/2 cup chopped nuts of your choice (optional)

1 1/2 cups granulated sugar
1 cup canned pumpkin
1/4 cup orange juice
1/2 tsp. baking powder
1/2 tsp. salt
1/2 tsp. cloves

Preheat oven to 350F. In a mixing bowl, cream butter and sugar. Add one egg. Beat thoroughly. Beat in second egg until smooth. Mix in pumpkin, rind and juice. In a separate bowl measure and mix all dry ingredients. Mix thoroughly with liquid ingredients. Pour into greased 9" x 5" bread pan. Bake for about 1 hour or until a toothpick inserted in the center of the loaf comes out clean. Cool in pan 10 minutes. Remove from pan.

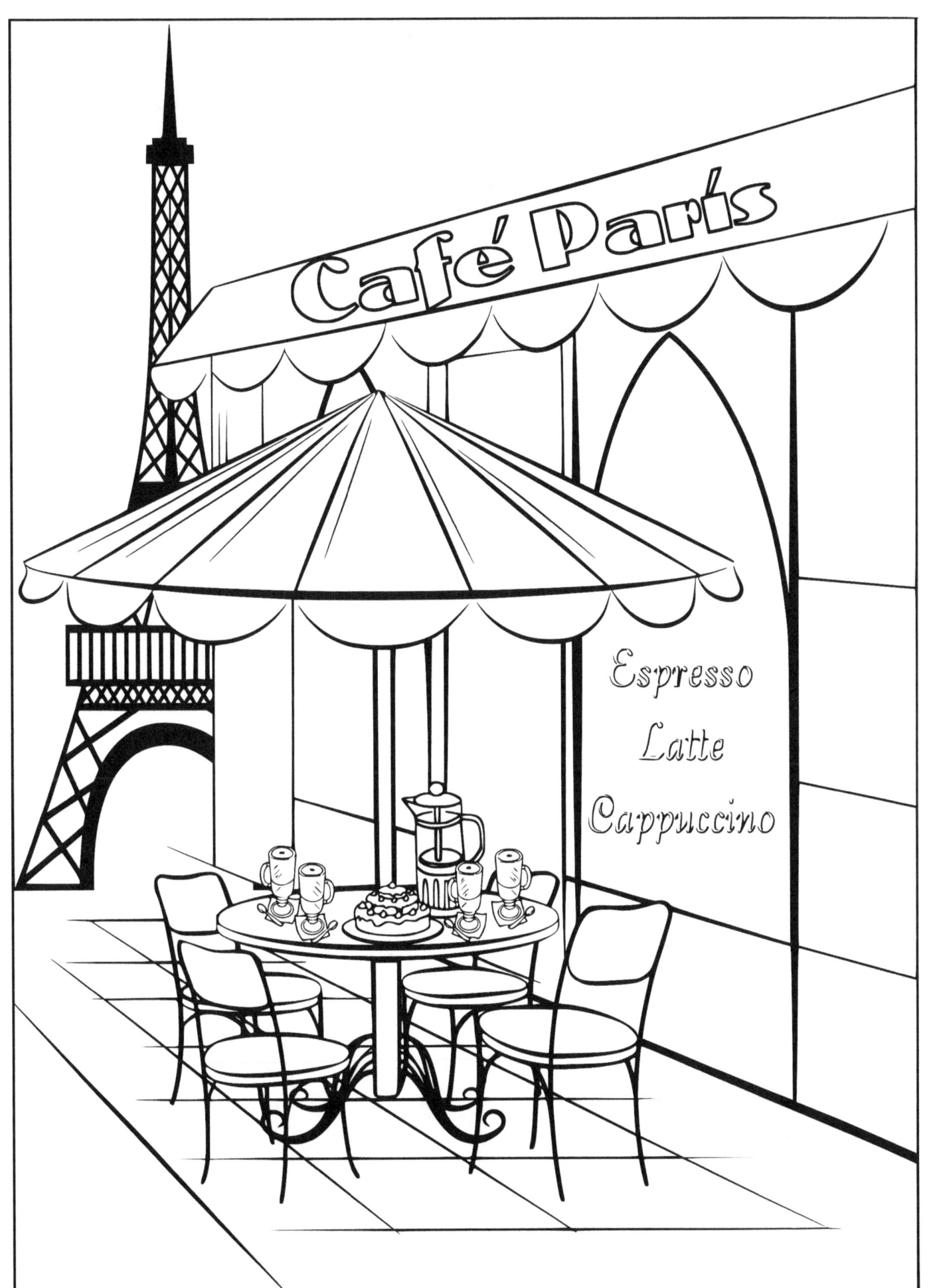

Fruited Yogurt Muffins

These muffins are moist and delicious. Use fresh fruit for best results. If using frozen berries drain them well before use.

2 cups all-purpose flour
1/3 cup granulated sugar
1 tsp. baking powder
1 tsp. baking soda
1/2 tsp. salt
1 1/2 cups finely chopped fresh fruit (such as strawberries)
1 1/4 cups plain yogurt
1/4 cup vegetable oil
1 tbsp. lemon juice
1 tsp. vanilla

Preheat oven to 375F. In a large bowl mix together dry ingredients. Toss fruit in flour mixture briefly. In a separate bowl mix liquid ingredients. Add the liquid to the flour mixture, stirring just to moisten. Fill greased muffin tins 2/3 full of batter. Bake 20 - 25 minutes or until golden brown.

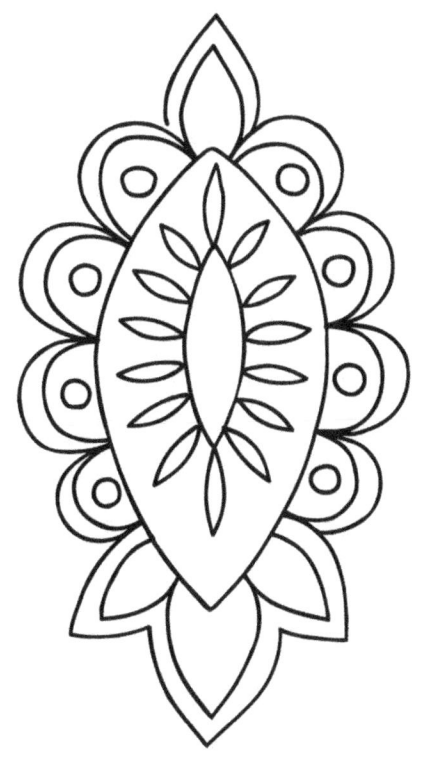

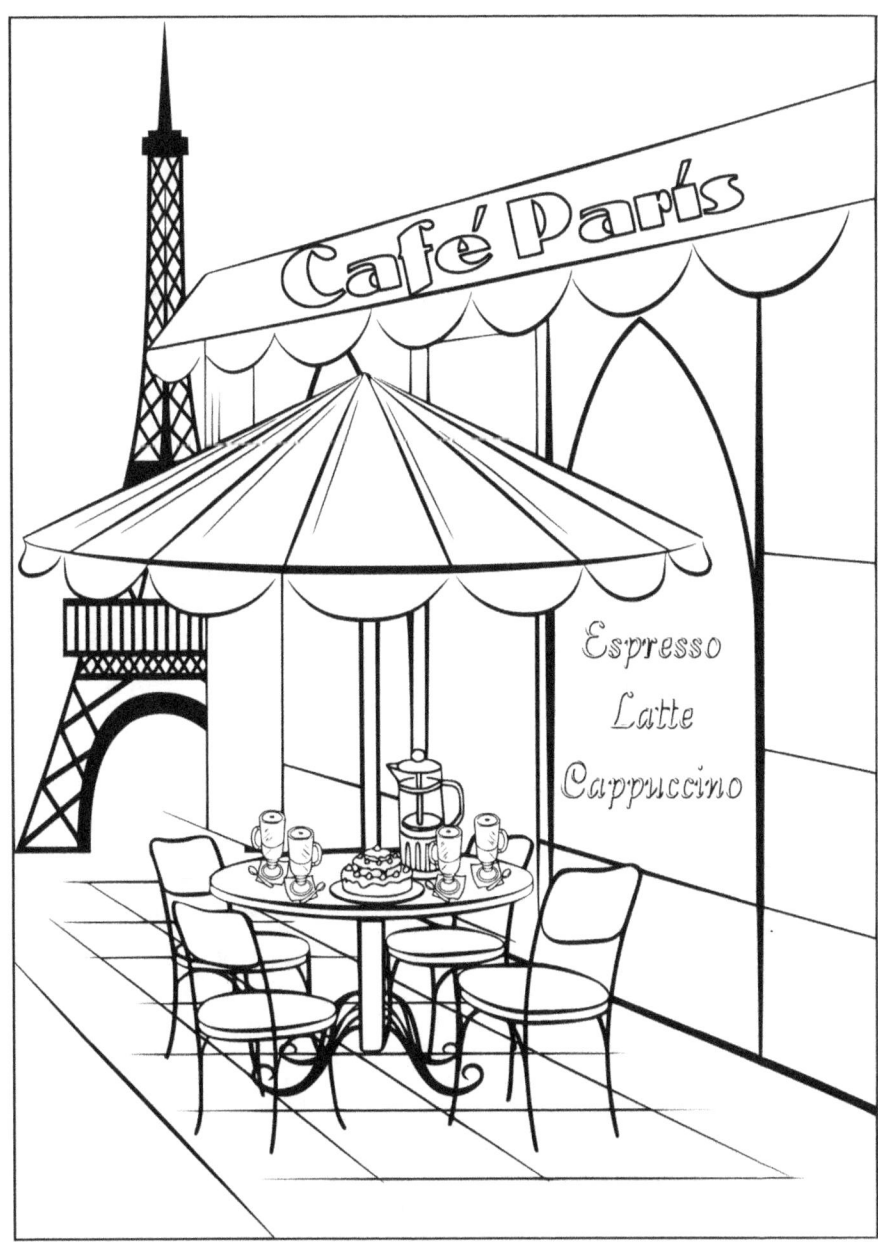

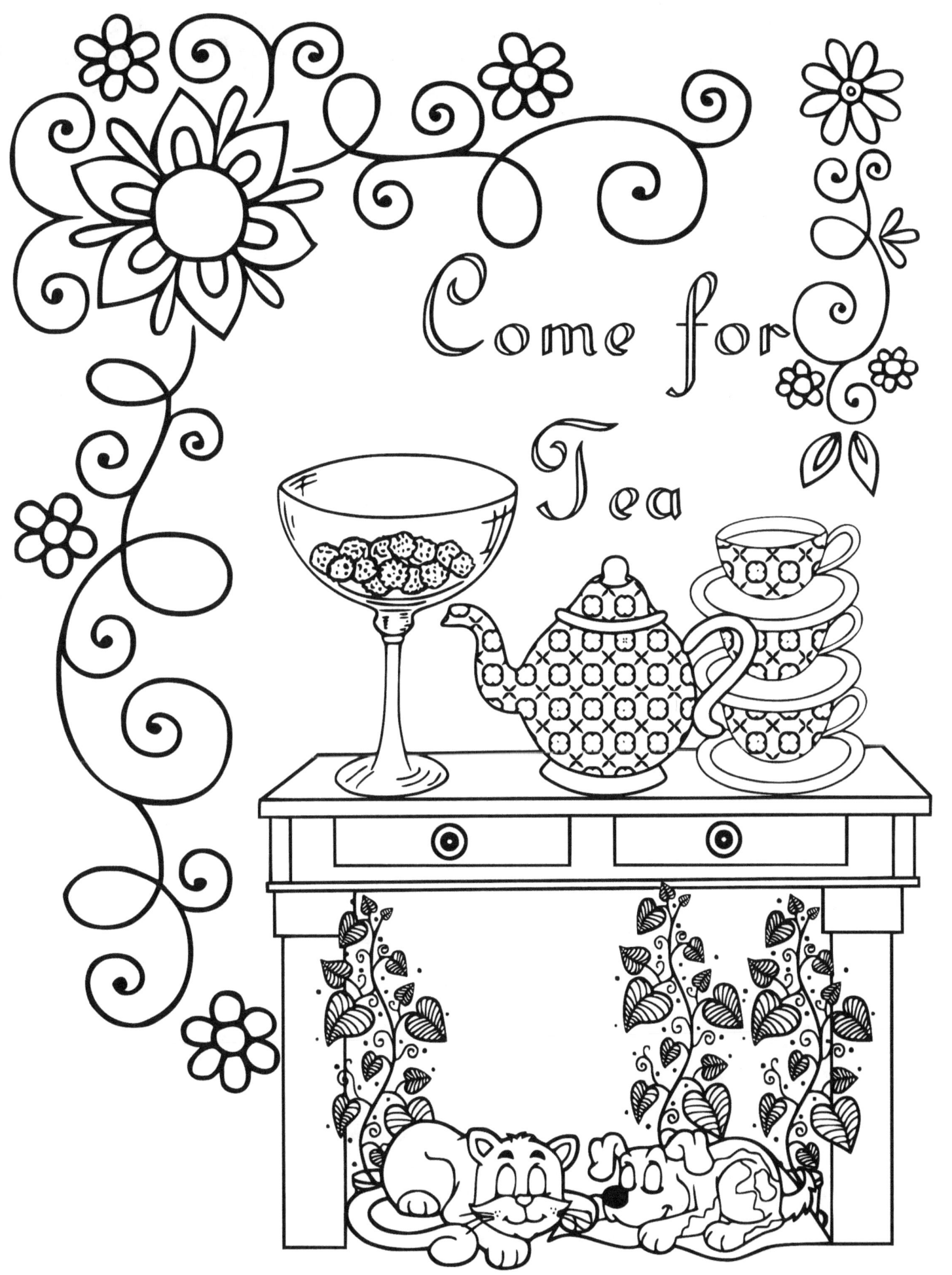

Come for Tea

There's nothing much more British than cucumber sandwiches. They can be dull and boring, or with a few added ingredients they can have such a fresh, apealing flavor that they are always well received. These are easy to make and just yummy.

1 seedless cucumber, thinly sliced
1/4 cup mayonnaise
1/4 tsp. salt
sprinkle of pepper

1/2 cup cream cheese, softened
1/2 tsp. lemon juice
1/4 tsp. dried dill
12 slices bread of your choice

Peel and slice cucumber. In a small bowl mix cream cheese, mayonnaise, lemon juice, salt, and dill. Spread lightly on the bread slices. Place cucumber on one side of the sandwich. Sprinkle with pepper. Top with second slice of bread, which has been spread with cheese mixture. Trim off crusts and cut sandwiches in smal pieces.

Cucumber Sandwiches

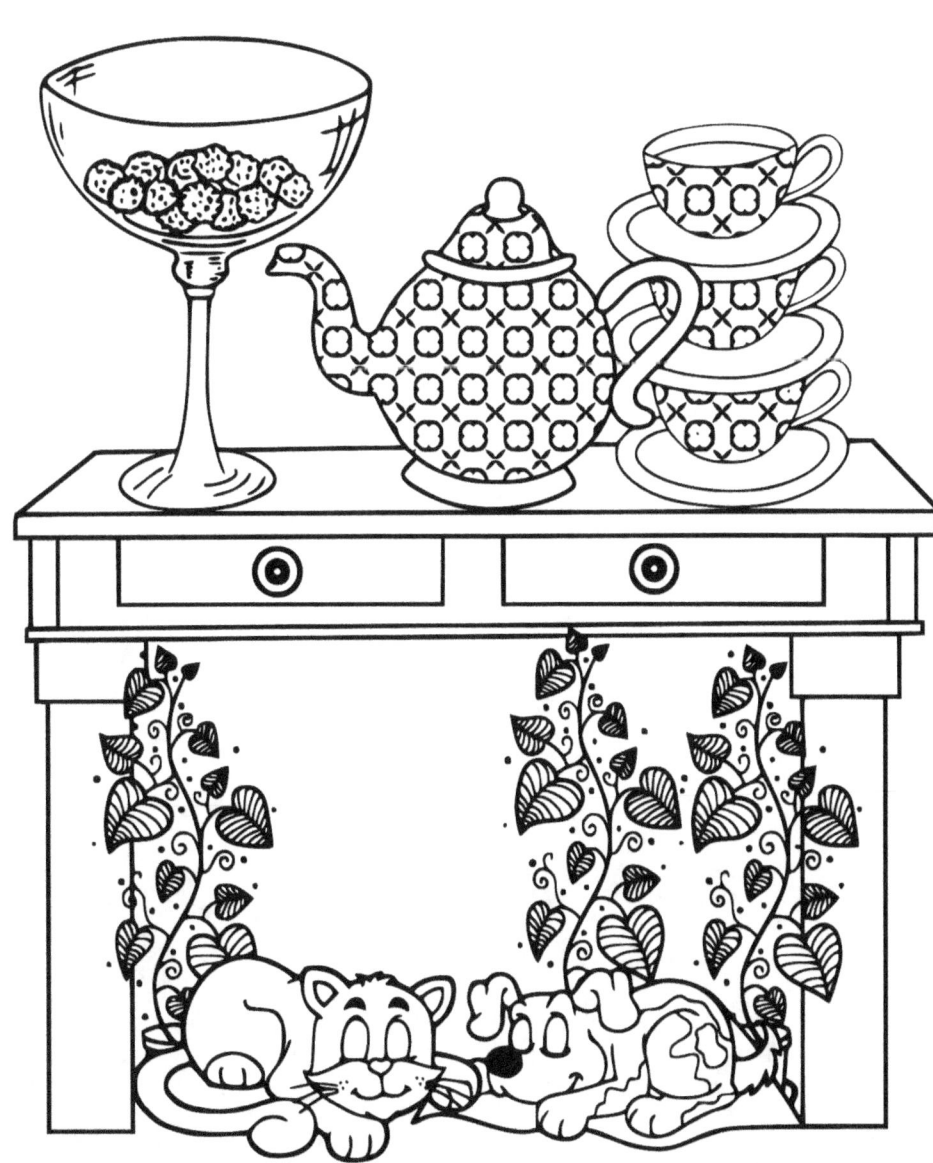

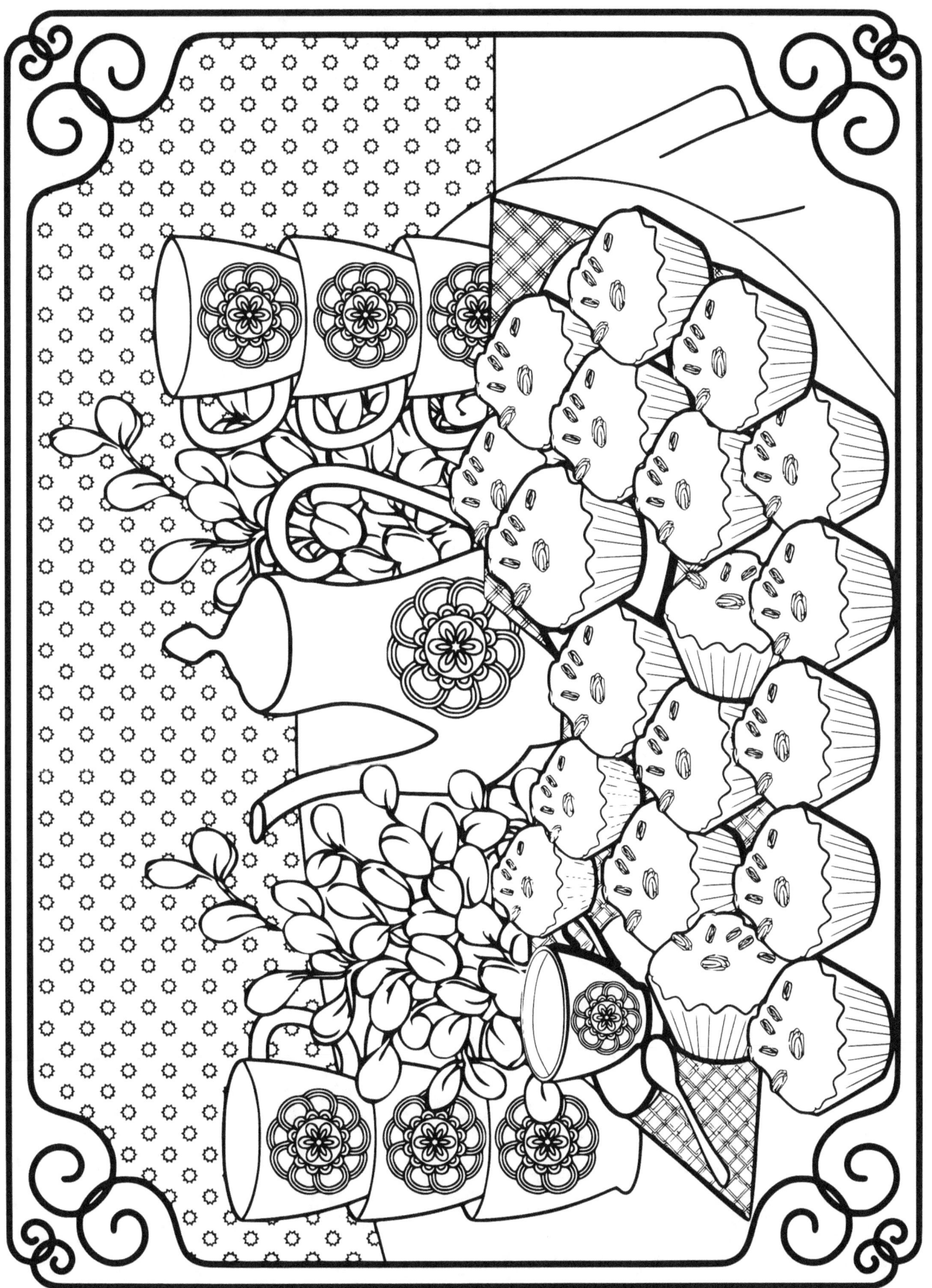

Cinnamon Swirl Muffins

These muffins are simply delicious. They're easy to make and great to serve with tea, coffee or milk. Easy to transport if you're going camping and they save well also. Your family will want you to make these often!

1/2 cup packed brown sugar
2 cups all-purpose flour
1/2 cup granulated sugar
2 eggs, well beaten
1 tsp. vanilla

2 tsp. cinnamon
1 tbsp. baking powder
1 tsp. salt
1 cup milk
1/4 cup vegetable oil

Preheat oven to 400F. Grease muffin tins. In a small bowl colmbine brown sugar and cinnamon. Set aside. In a large bowl combine dry ingredients. Mix thoroughly. Make a well in the center. In a separate bowl comine liquid ingredients. Pour liquid ingredients in the well of dry ingredients. Stir until just moistened. Fill muffin tins 2/3 full. Sprinkle with cinnamon mixture. Bake 15 - 17 minutes or until a toothpick inserted in the center of a muffin comes out clean.

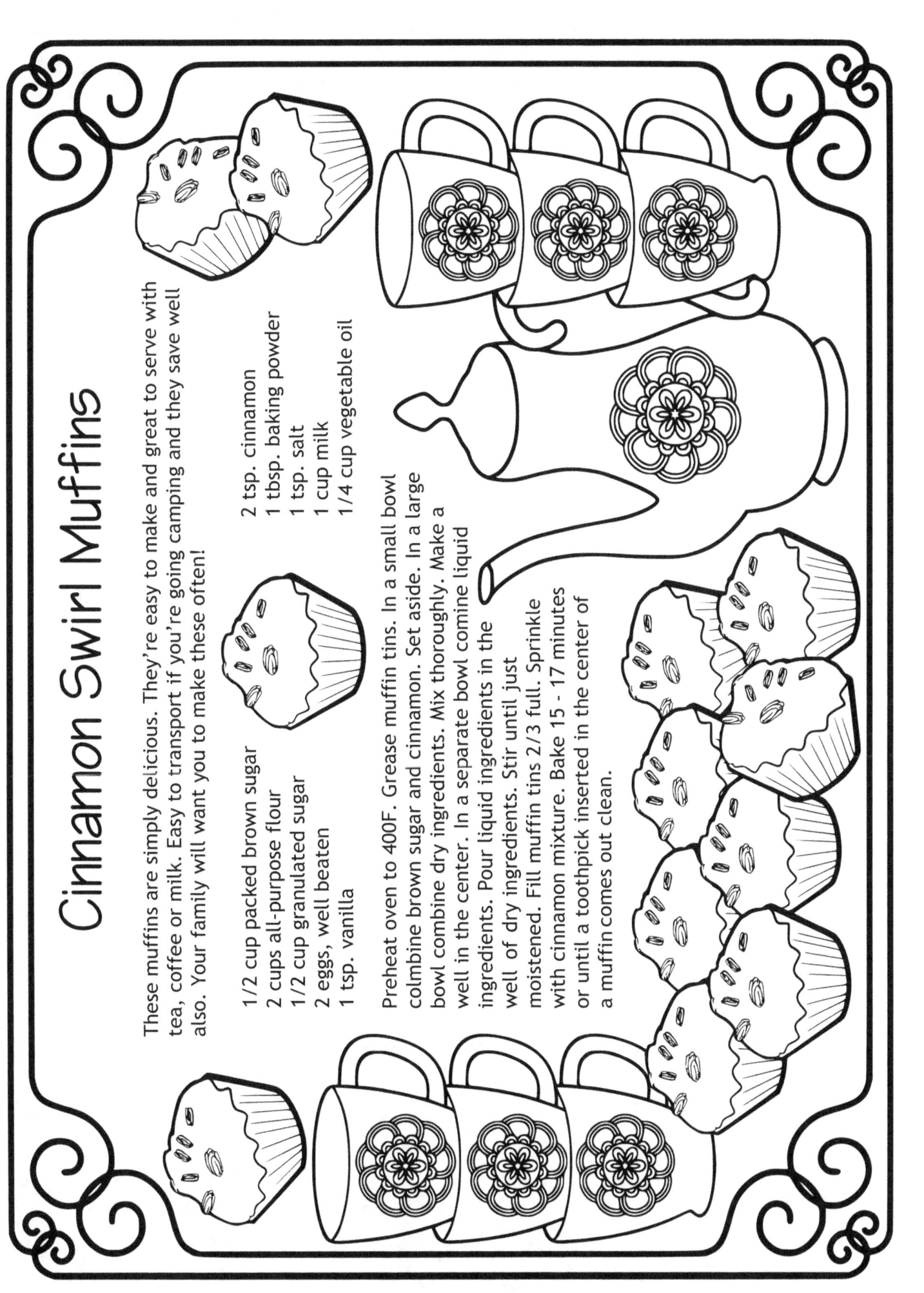

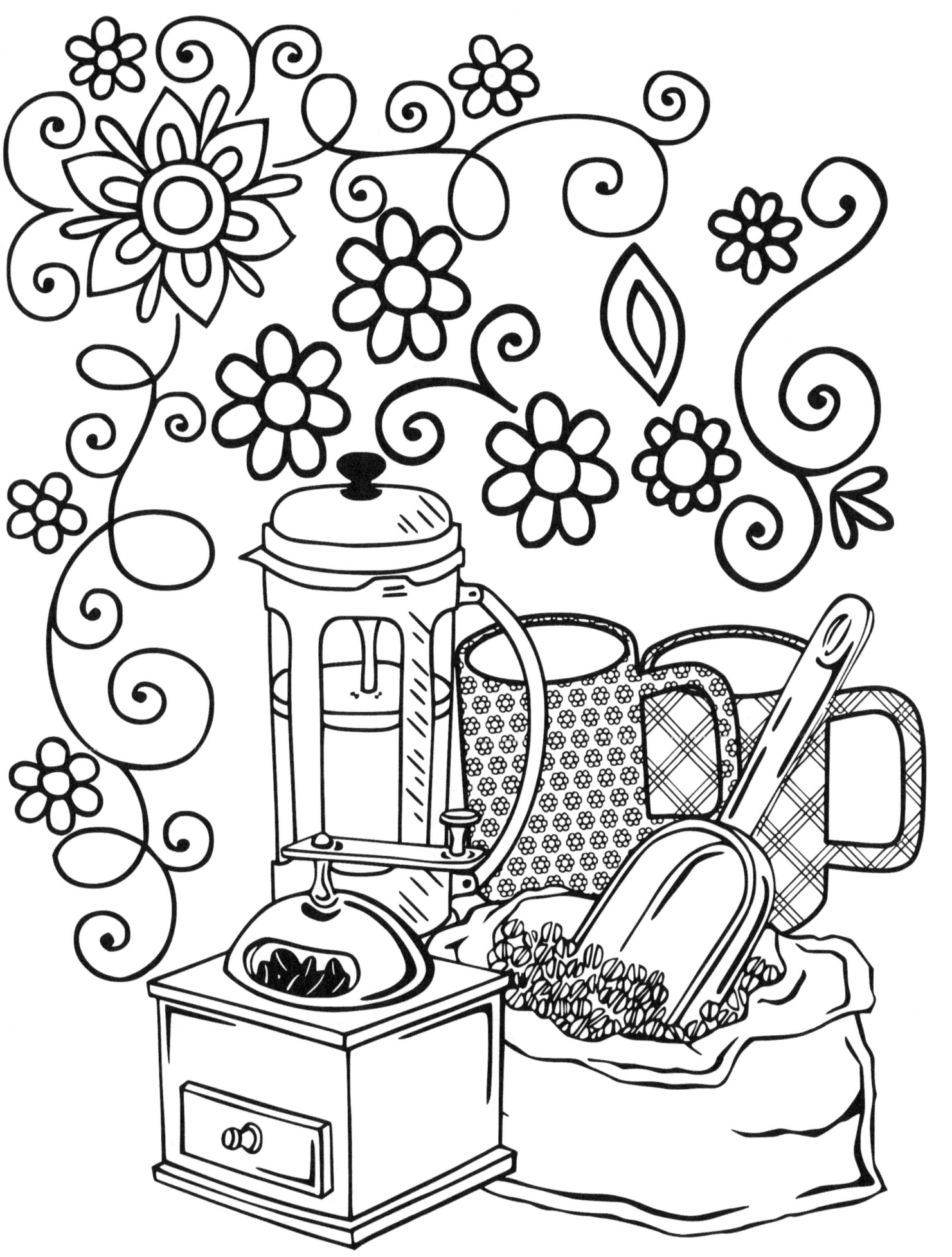

Best Ever Coffee Cake

This coffee cake looks really pitted but that's the way it's supposed to look. However, it is moist and delicious and people always come back for more. Served with a steaming cup of coffee and some butter, it's a winner every time.

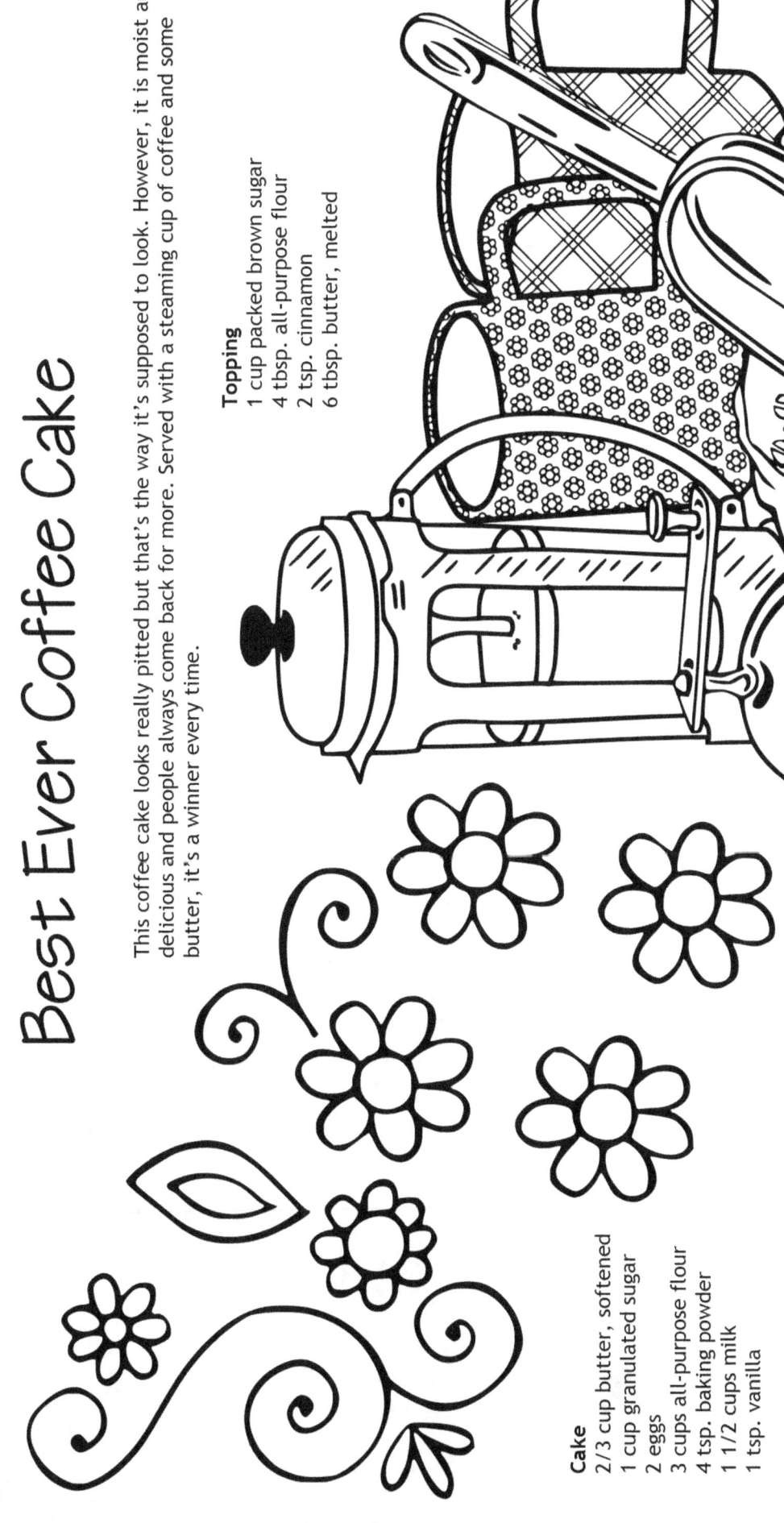

Topping
1 cup packed brown sugar
4 tbsp. all-purpose flour
2 tsp. cinnamon
6 tbsp. butter, melted

Cake
2/3 cup butter, softened
1 cup granulated sugar
2 eggs
3 cups all-purpose flour
4 tsp. baking powder
1 1/2 cups milk
1 tsp. vanilla

Preheat oven to 375F. Butter a 9" x 13" baking dish and set aside. For topping: mix all ingredients together. Set aside. For cake: cream butter sugar and egg together in a large bowl. In a separate bowl combine dry ingredients. Add vanilla to milk. Add alternately with flour mixture to butter mixture. Stir after each addition until batter is smooth. Pour into baking dish and smooth top. Using fingers for easy distribution, sprinkle topping over batter. Bake for about 35 minutes or until a toothpick inserted in the center of the cake comes out clean. Best served warm but still delicious cool as well.

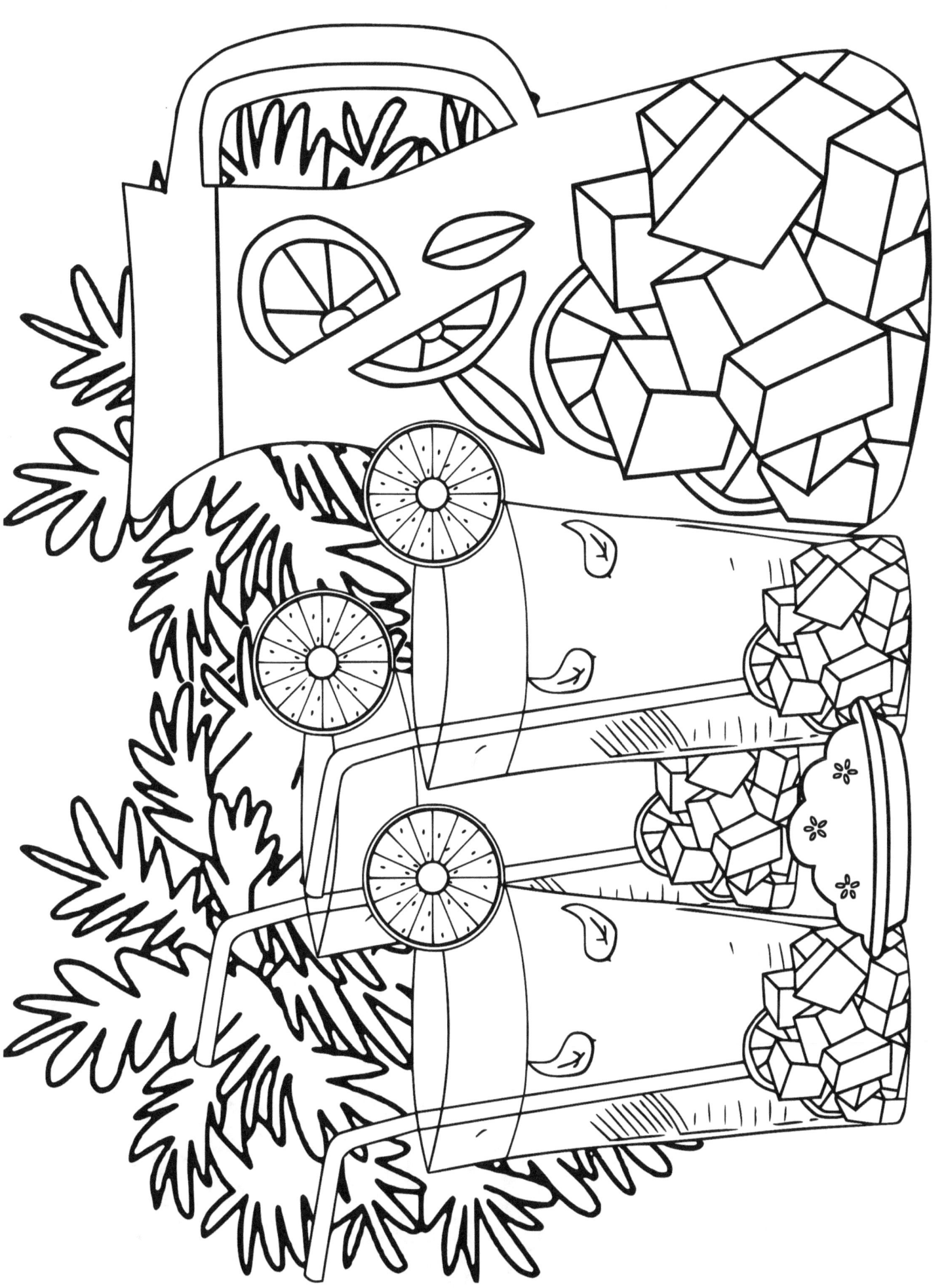

Honey Carrot Cookies

When our kids were all living at home I couldn't keep these cookies around at all. Our youngest daughter thought they were the best. A soft, cake-like cookie with marvellous flavor. Top with cream cheese frosting for a real treat.

3/4 cup butter or margarine
1/2 cup soft honey
1/2 tsp. vanilla
1/2 tsp. baking soda
1 tsp. cinnamon
1 3/4 cups all-purpose flour

1/4 cup packed brown sugar
2 eggs
1 tsp. baking powder
1/2 tsp. salt
1 cup grated carrot

Grease cookie sheets. Preheat over to 350F. In a large bowl cream butter and sugar. Stir in honey. Add eggs and beat well. Stir in vanilla, baking powder, baking soda, salt and cinnamon. Stir in grated carrot. Gradually mix in flour. Drop by teaspoonfuls on cookie sheets. Allow at least 2" between each cookie as they tend to spread. Bake on middle rack for 10 to 12 minutes. When cool, frost with Cream Cheese Frosting recipe below.

Cream Cheese Frosting: Mix 4 oz. cream cheese, room temperature and 1/4 cup soft butter together. Stir in 1 tsp. vanilla. Add 1-1 1/2 cups icing sugar and mix until thoroughly blended. Spread over cooled cookies.

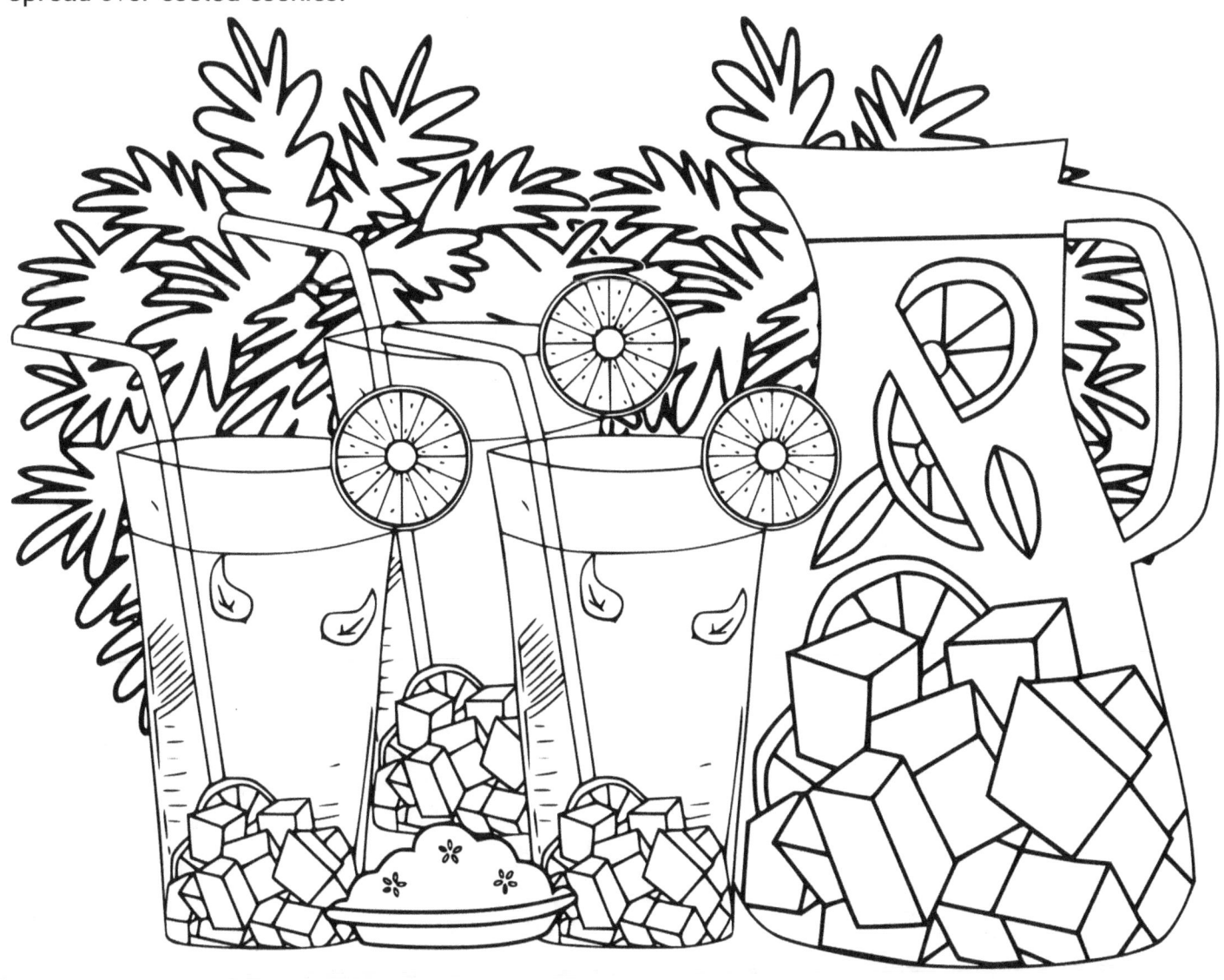

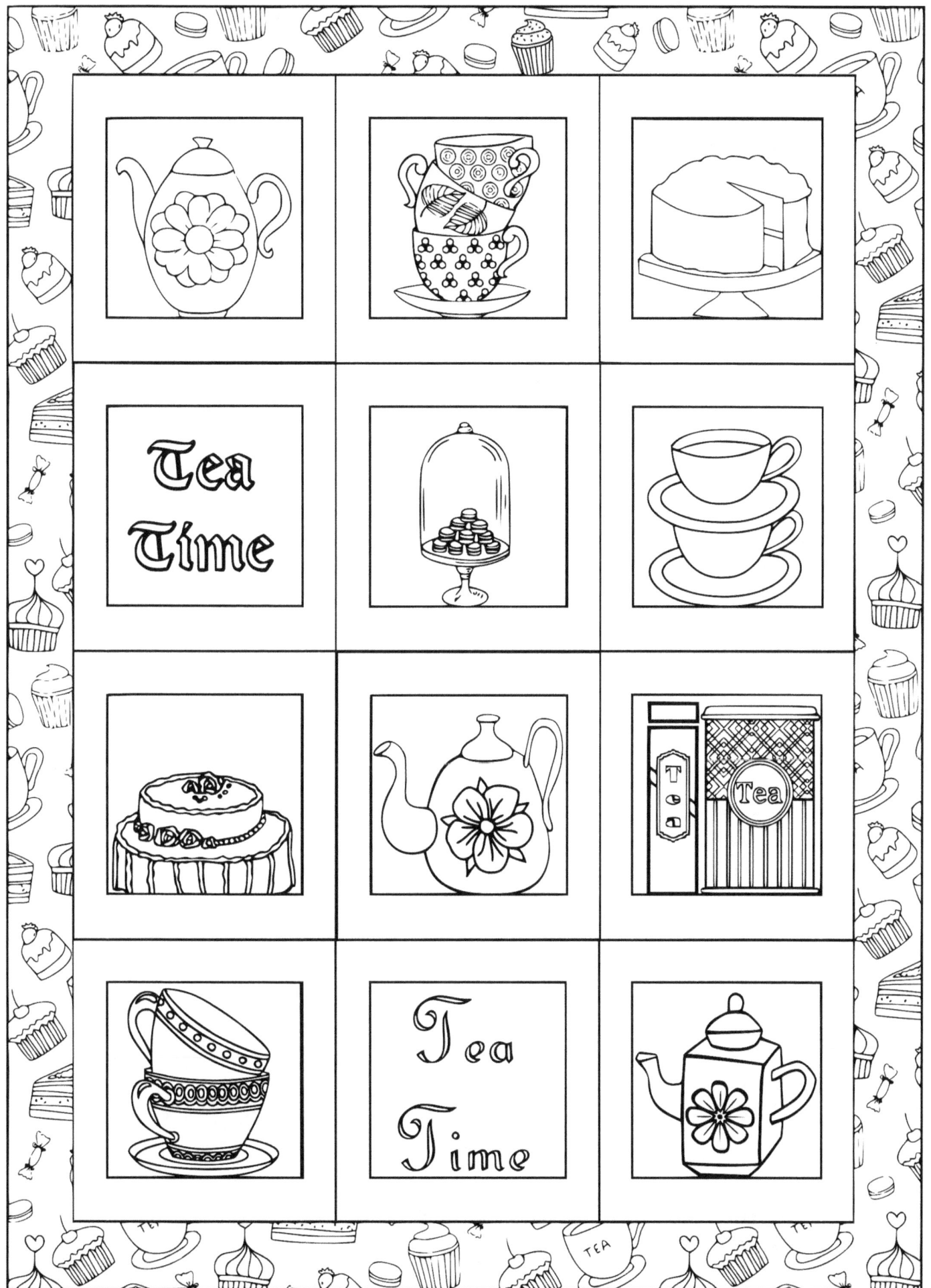

Shrimp in a Basket

Even though this recipe has a long list of ingredients it's well worth making. It has a delicate, subtle flavor and great visual appeal. Perfect for afternoon tea.

2 tbsp. vegetable oil
1/4 cup diced celery
1 garlic clove, minced
2 lbs. cooked shrimmp
1/2 tsp. basil
1/2 tsp. pepper
2 tbsp. cornstarch
6 large puff pastry shells

1/4 cup julienne carrots
1/4 cup diced red pepper
1/2 cup white wine*
6 tbsp. chopped parsley
1/2 tsp. salt
1/2 cup whipping cream
1/4 cup water
paprika

* You can substitute non-alcoholic apple cider

Heat vegetable oil in a large frying pan. Stir-fry carrots, celery and red pepper for about 5 minutes or until they are just tender-crisp. Add wine, shrimp and seasonings. Cover and bring to a boil. In a small bowl mix cornstarch and water. Gradually add to shrimp mixture to thicken, stirring constantly. Use only enough of the thickening liquid to achieve the desired consistency. Continue to cook for about 5 minutes, stirring almost constantly. Spoon into puff pastry shells and sprinkle with paprika. Serve warm.

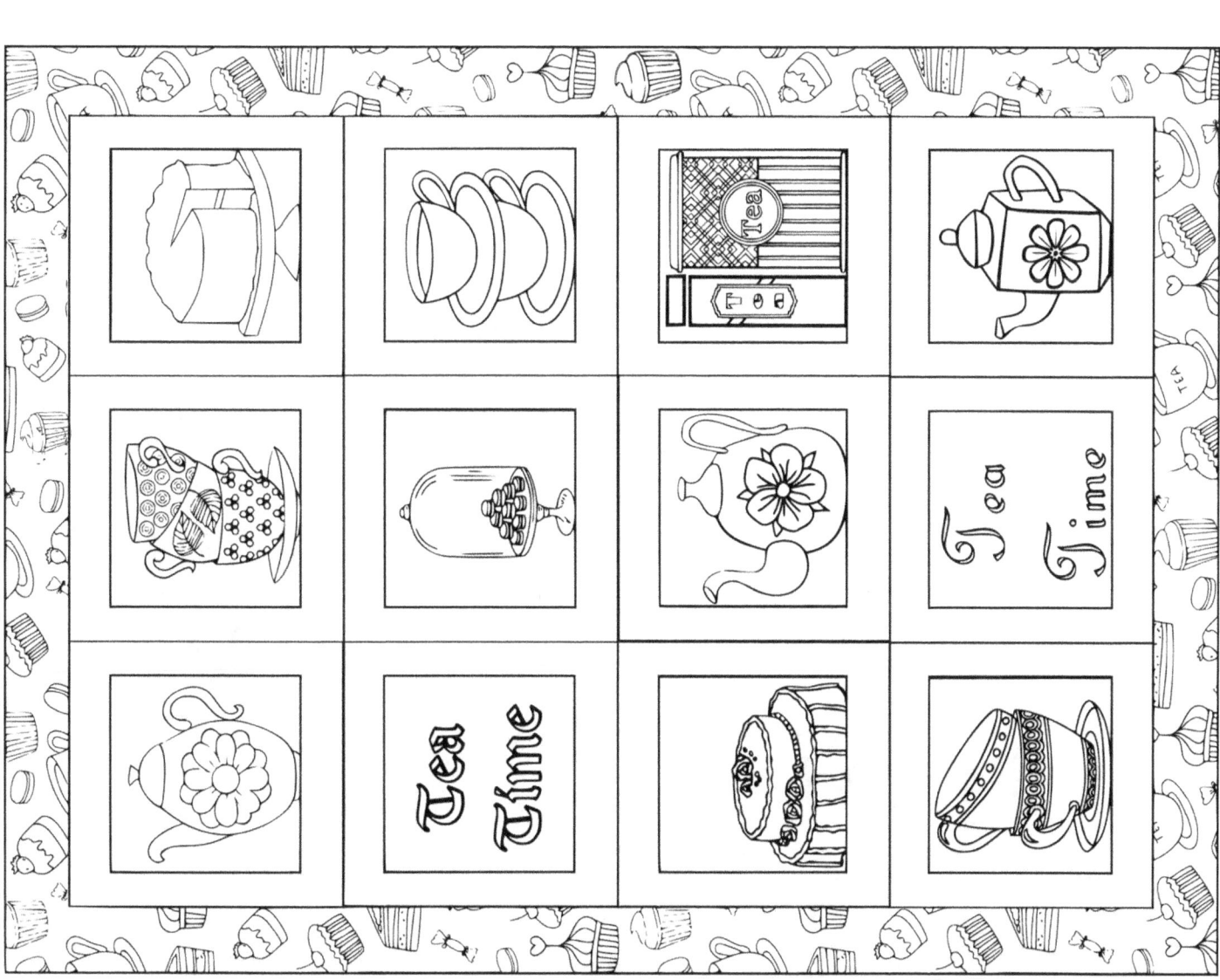

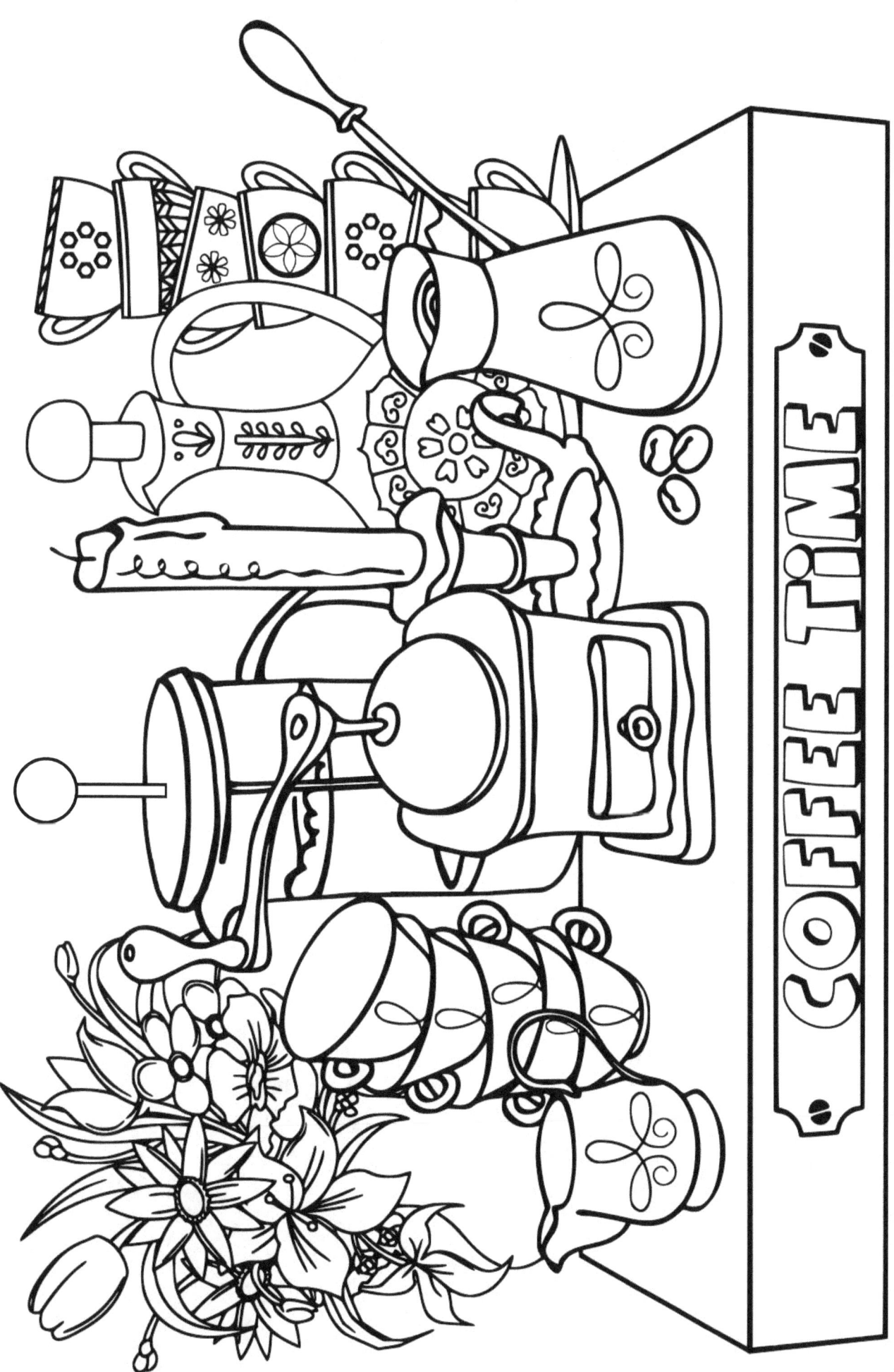

Banana Pecan Bread

This all-time favorite has rich flavor and is simply delicious served with butter. You can also spread it with a thin layer of strawberry jam and/or a bit of peanut butter for some interesting flavors. Easy to make and it never seems to fail.

1/2 cup butter or margarine	1 cup granulated sugar
2 eggs, slightly beaten	1 cup mashed, ripe bananas
2 cups all-purpose flour	1 tsp. baking soda
1 tsp. baking powder	1/2 tsp. salt

1/2 cup chopped pecans

Preheat oven to 350F. In a large bowl cream butter and sugar together. Beat in eggs, one at a time, beating until smooth. Add mashed banana and mix well. In a separate bowl, mix dry ingredients. Make a well in the center and pour liquid mixture into well. Stir only until moistened. Fold in pecans. Pour into a greased 9" x 5" bread pan. Bake for about 1 hour or until a toothpick inserted in the middle of the loaf comes out clean. Let stand 10 minutes. Remove from pan and place on cake rack to cool.

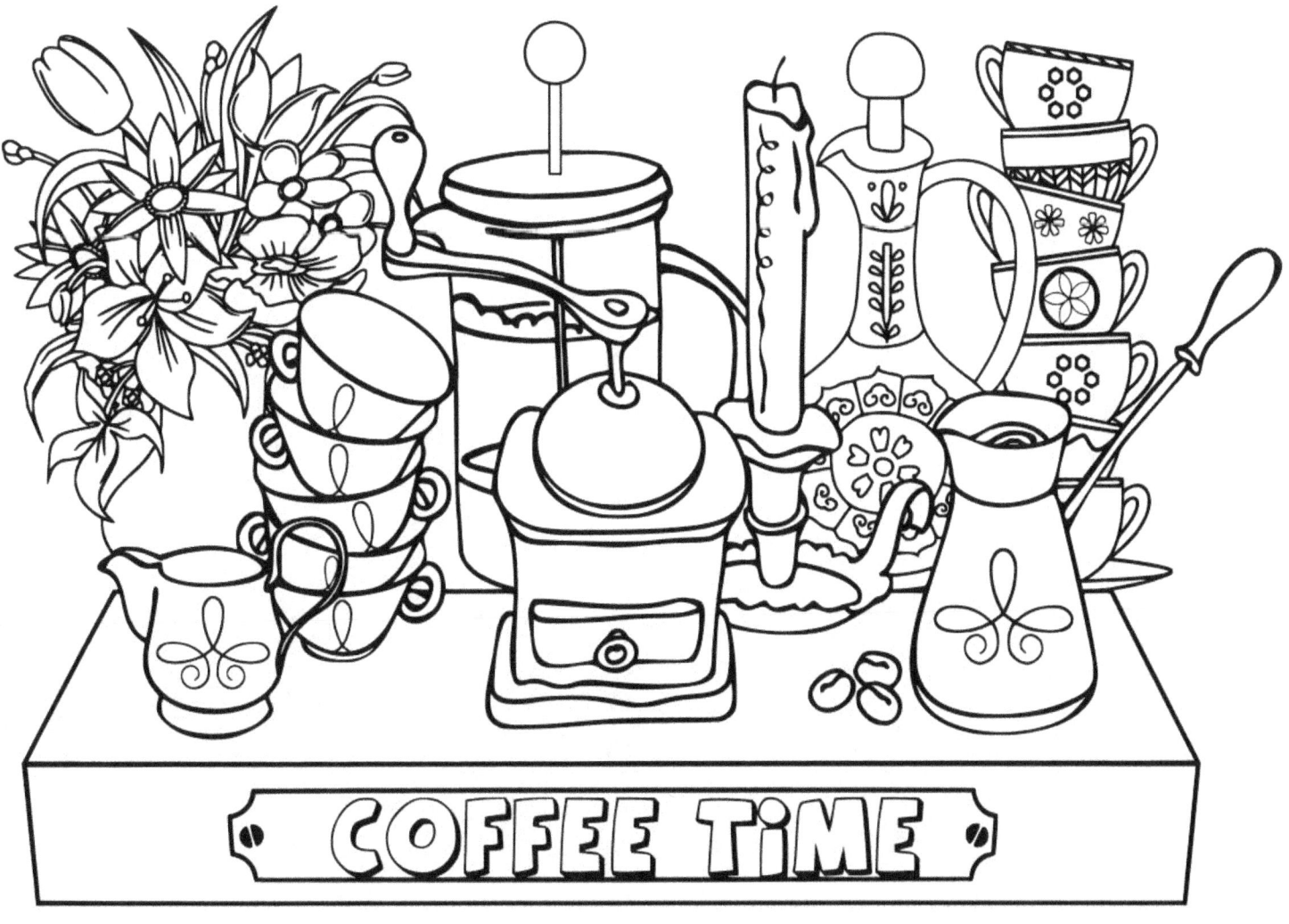

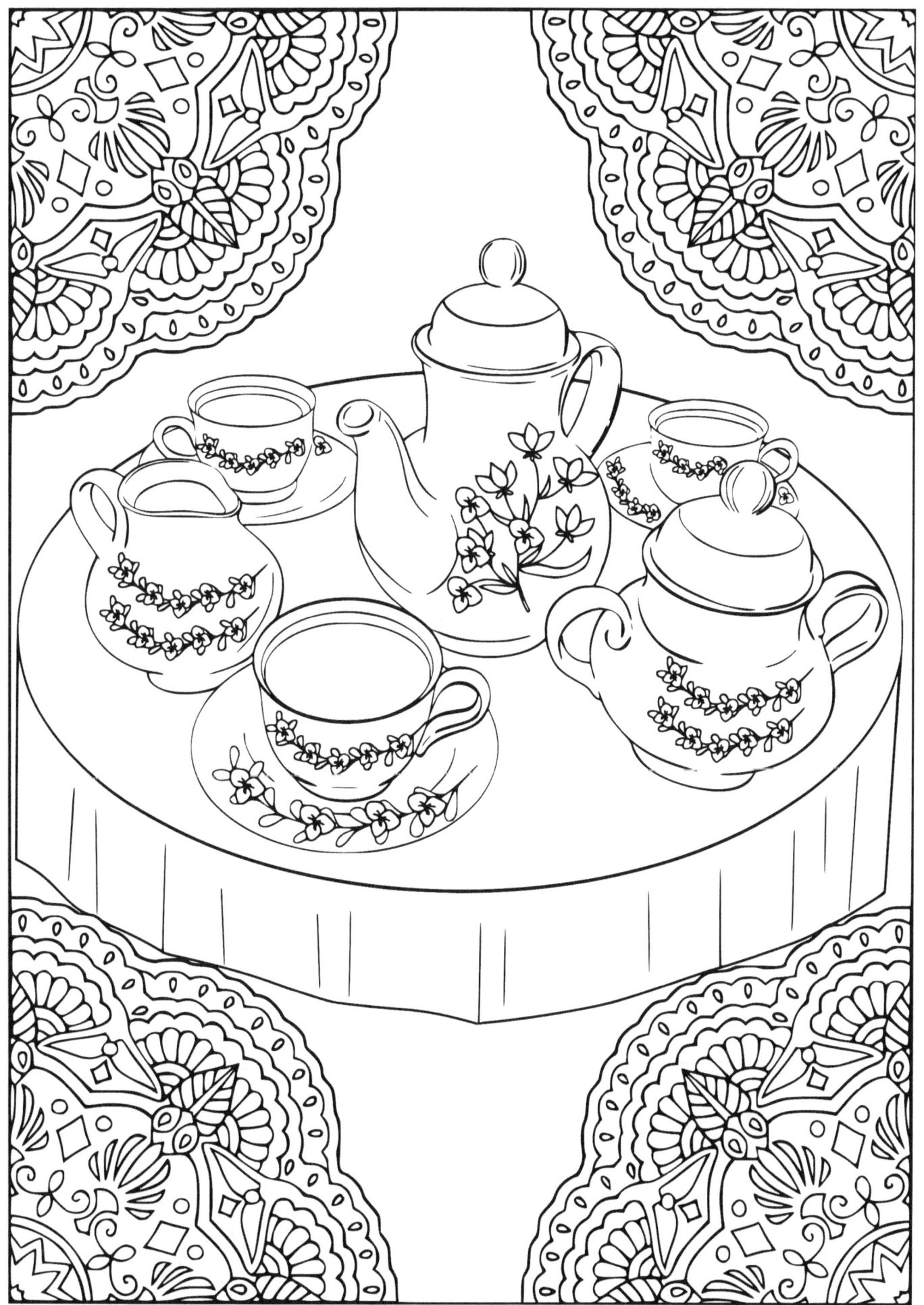

Gingered Scones

I know there's already a scone recipe in this book but this recipe is so good I just had to include it. And it's quite different from a regular scone as well. Served with marmalade or apricot jam, this is a truly delicious scone to enjoy with tea.

2 cups all-purpose flour
3 tsp. baking powder
1/2 tsp. baking soda
1/2 tsp. cinnamon
1 beaten egg yolk
1/4 cup milk

2 tbsp. brown sugar
1 tsp. ginger
1/2 tsp. salt
1/4 cup butter
1/3 cup molasses
1 slightly beaten egg white

Preheat oven to 400F. Combine dry ingredients in a bowl and mix thoroughly. Using a pastry blender, cut in butter till mixture resembles coarse crumbs. Make a well in the center. In a separate bowl, stir together egg yolk, molasses and milk. Pour into well in center of dry ingredients. Stir with a fork to combine. Turn dough onto a lightly floured surface. Quicklly knead dough 10 to 12 strokes. Pat dough out until it is about 3/4" thick. Cut into wedges. Arrange wedges 1" apart on an ungreased baking sheet. Brush with egg white. Bake for 12 to 15 minutes or until golden brown. Cool on a wire rack. Serve warm.

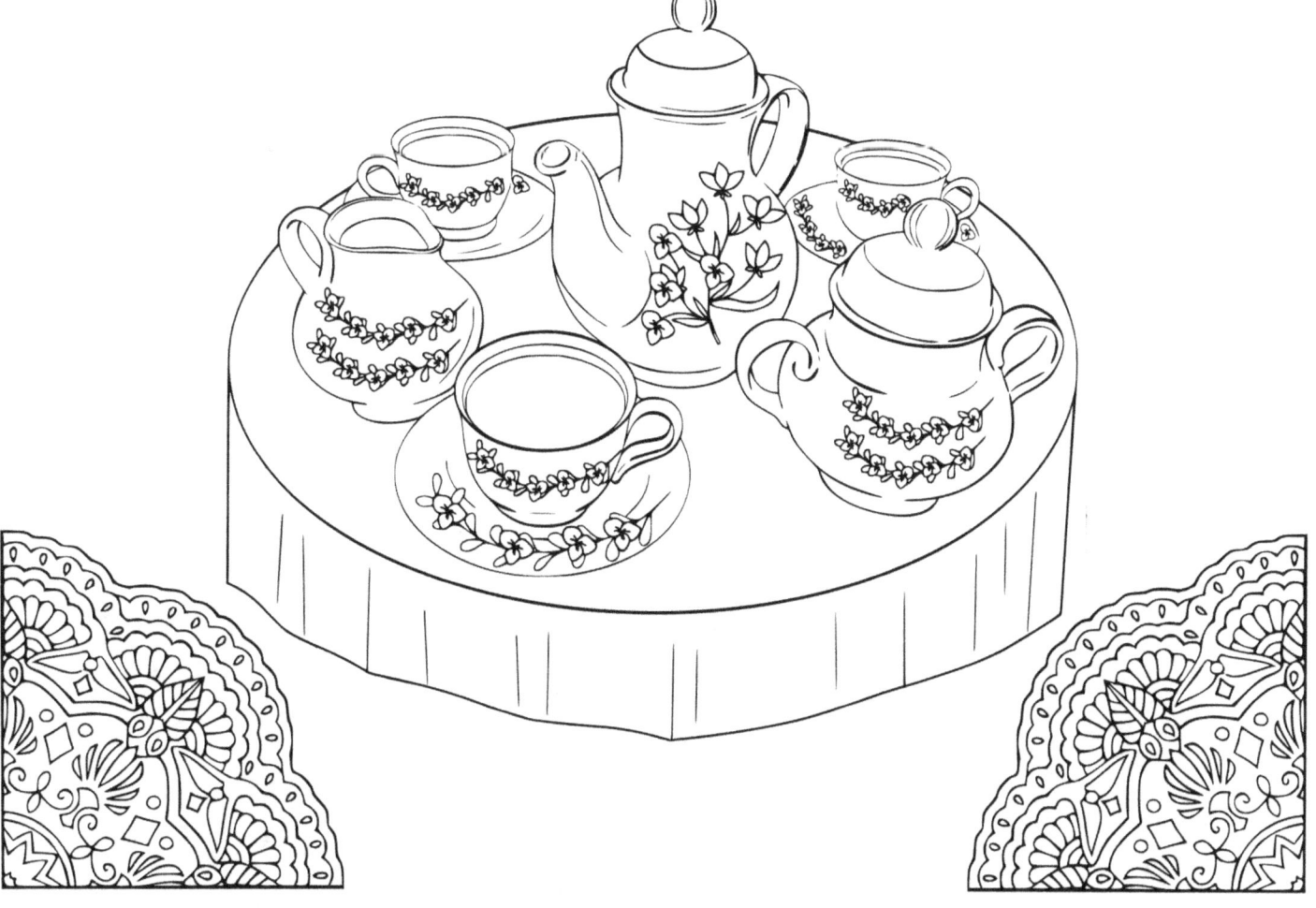

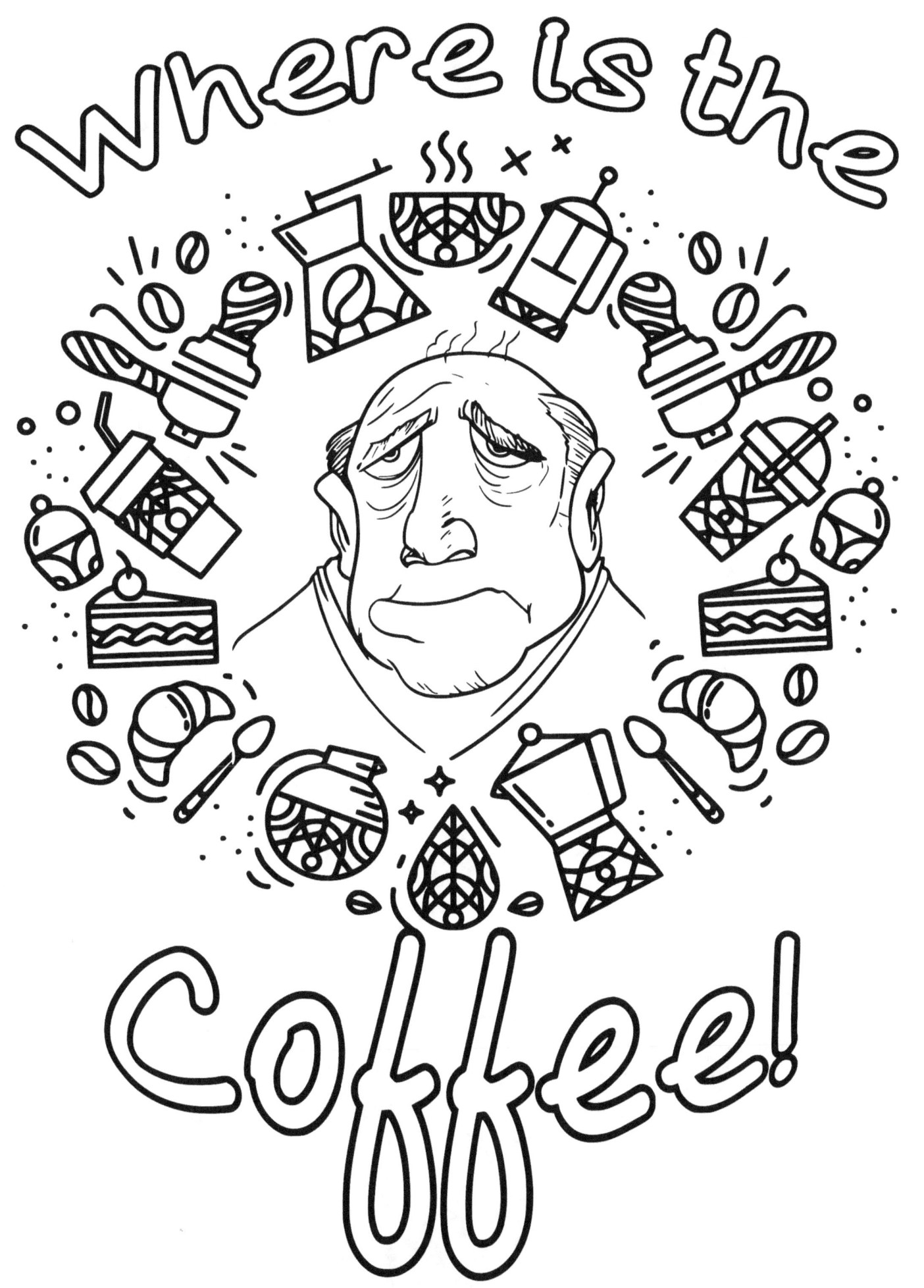

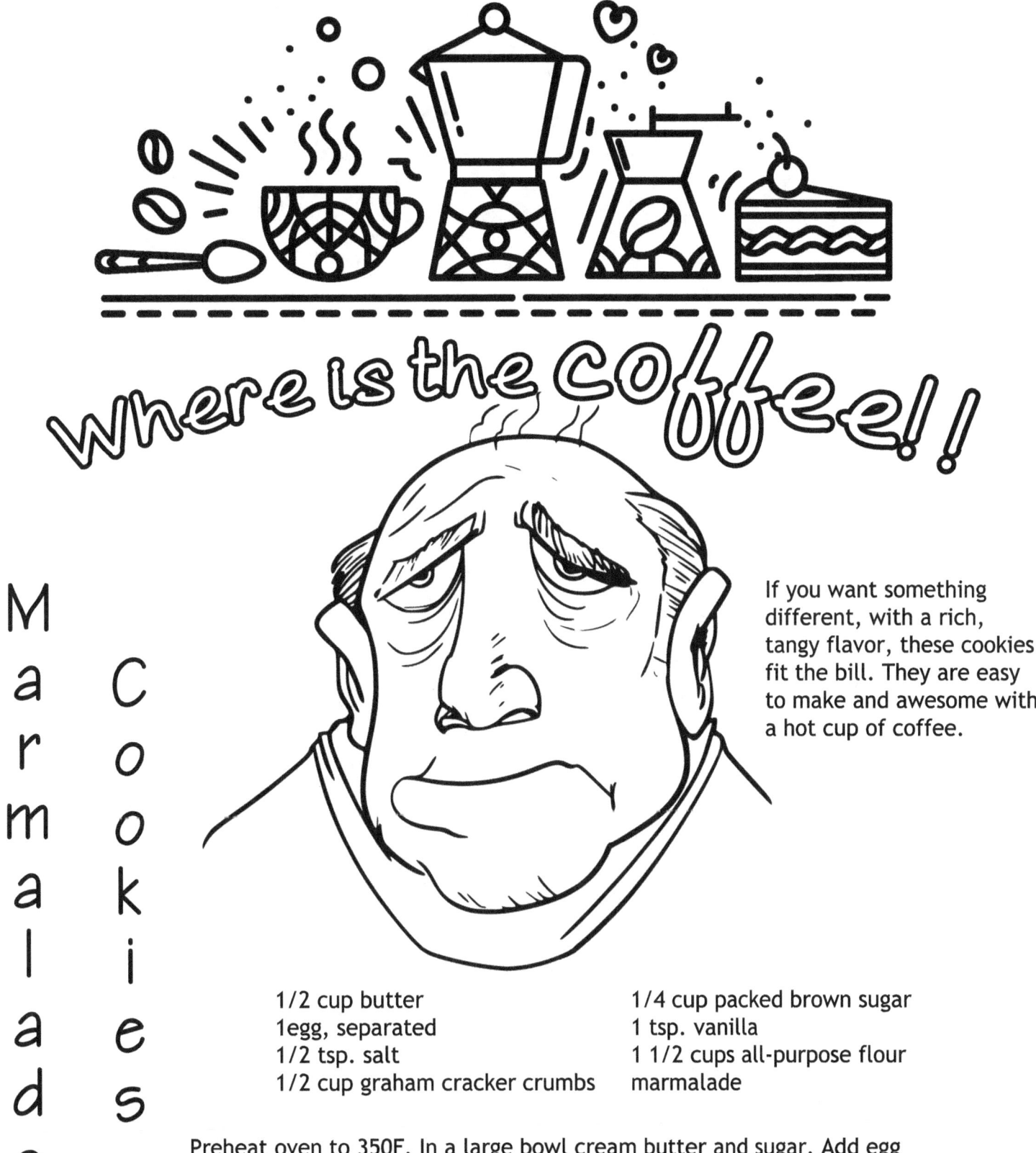

Where is the coffee!!

Marmalade Cookies

If you want something different, with a rich, tangy flavor, these cookies fit the bill. They are easy to make and awesome with a hot cup of coffee.

1/2 cup butter
1egg, separated
1/2 tsp. salt
1/2 cup graham cracker crumbs

1/4 cup packed brown sugar
1 tsp. vanilla
1 1/2 cups all-purpose flour
marmalade

Preheat oven to 350F. In a large bowl cream butter and sugar. Add egg yolk and beat thoroughly. Stir in vanilla and salt. Gradually mix in flour.. Form dough into 1" balls and dip in slightly beaten egg white. Roll in graham cracker crumbs. Place on ungreased cookie sheet. Gently press a finger into the center of each ball to make a hollow. Fill hollows with marmalade. Bake for 12 to 15 minutes or until cookies are golden brown.

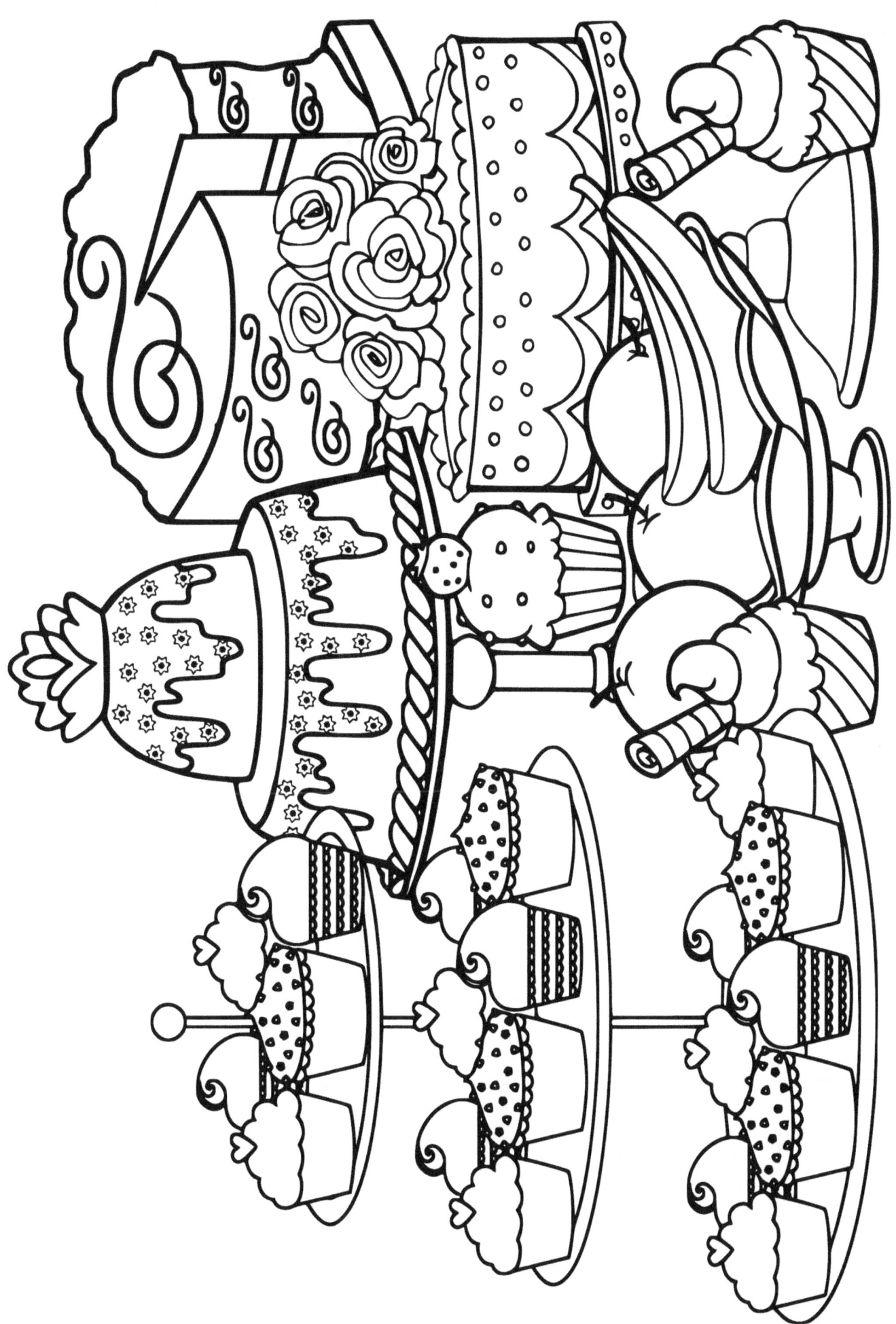

Cranberry Orange Loaf

Truly yummy and a real crowd pleaser. You might want to consider doubling this recipe so you have two loaves instead of just one.

1/4 cup butter or margarine
1 cup granulated sugar
1 egg
juice of one orange + enough water to make 3/4 cup
1 tsp. vanilla
2 cups all-purpose flour
1 1/2 tsp. baking powder
1/2 tsp. baking soda
1/2 tsp. salt
grated rind of one orange
1 1/2 cups cranberries cut in halves

Preheat oven to 350F. Put butter, sugar and egg in mixing bowl. Beat until smooth. Stir in juice and vanilla. In a second bowl combine dry ingredients. Make a well in center. Pour liquid ingredients into well and mix until just moistened. Fold in cranberries.

Pour batter into greased 9" x 5" bread pan. Bake for 1 hour or until a toothpick inserted in the center of loaf comes out clean.

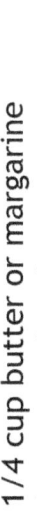
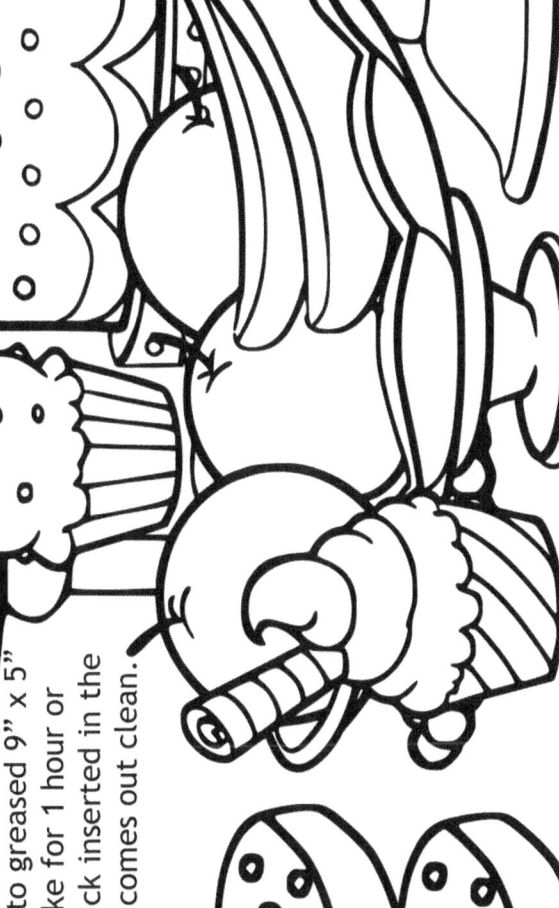

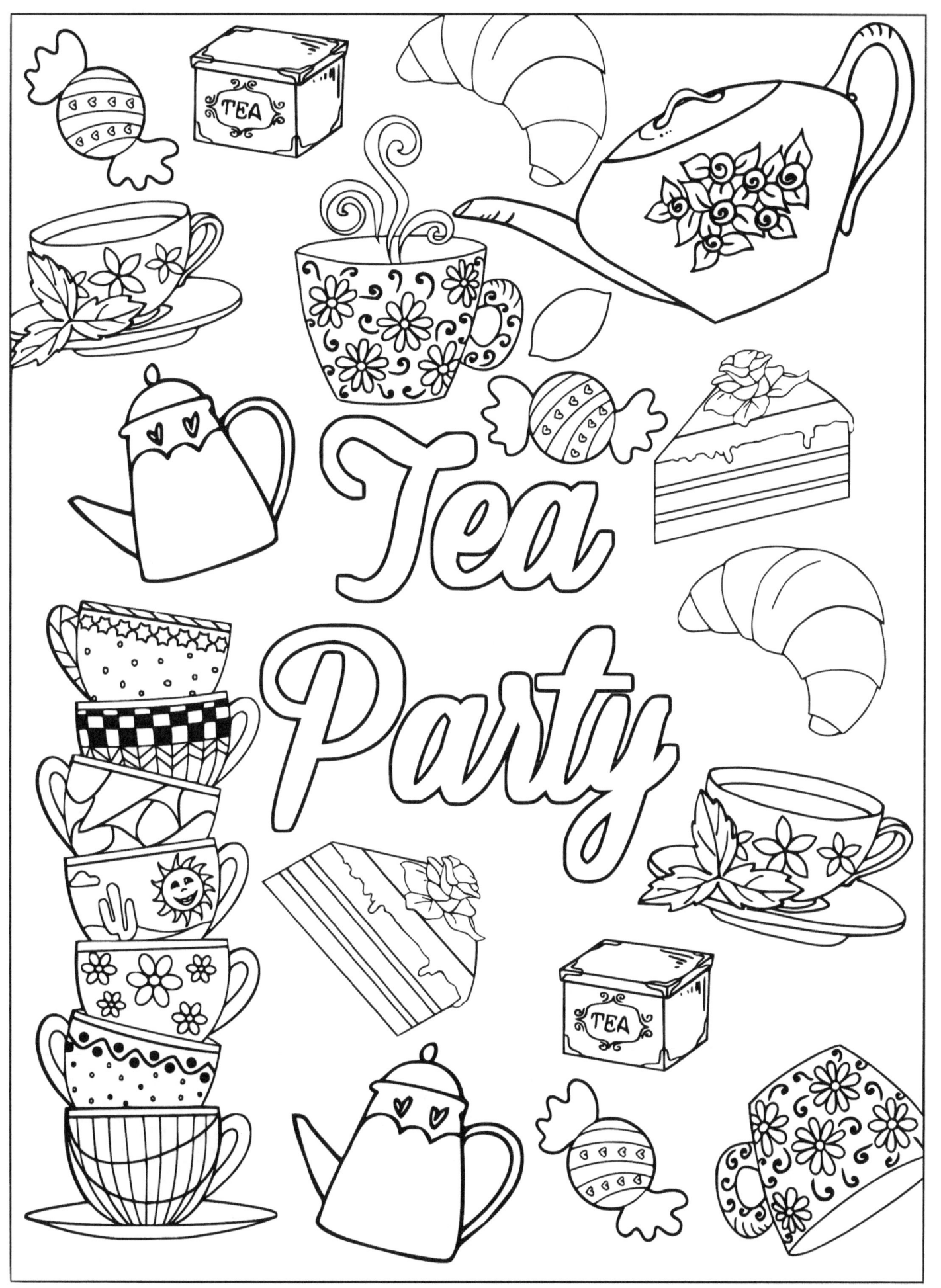

Individual Oreo® Cheesecakes

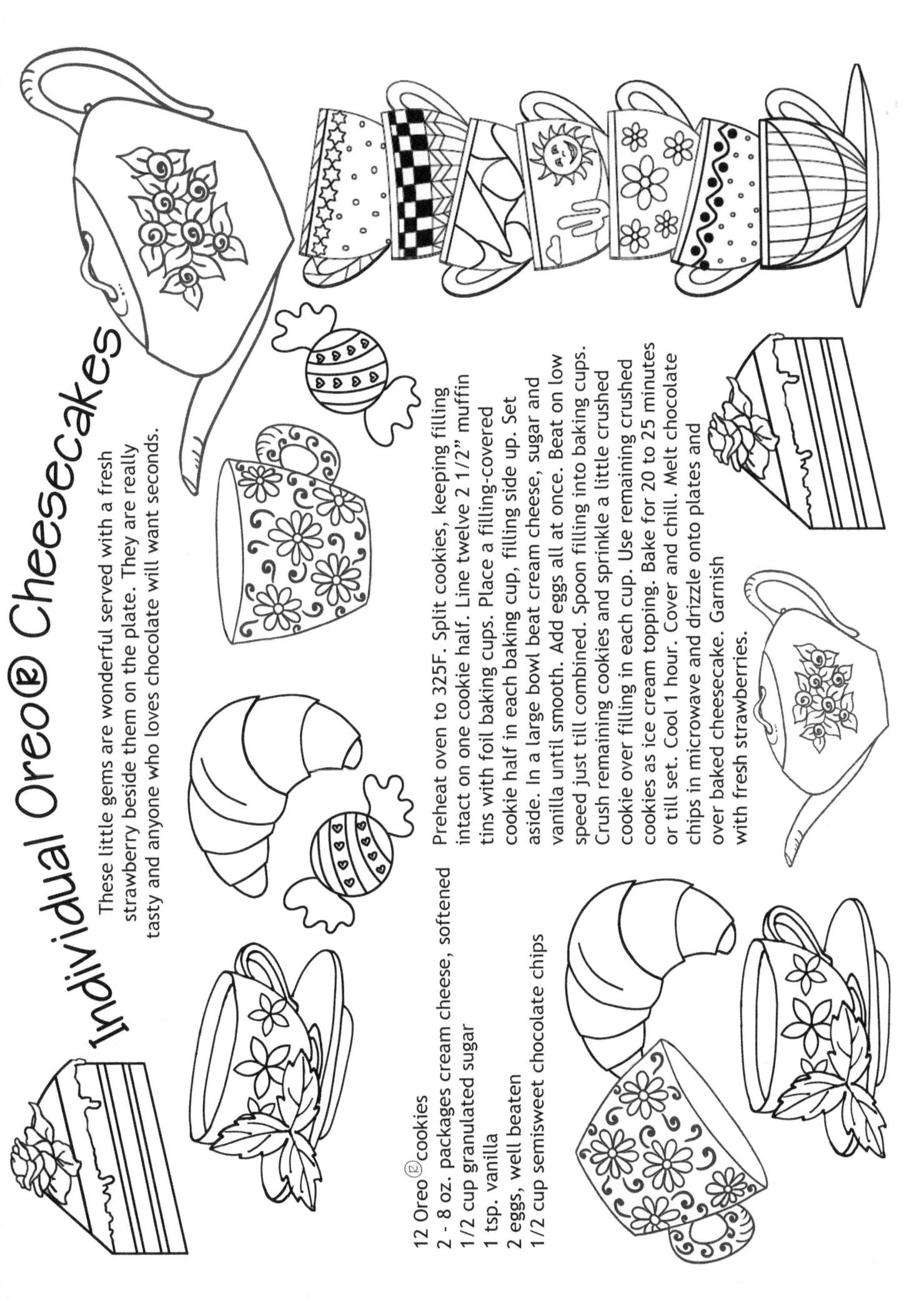

These little gems are wonderful served with a fresh strawberry beside them on the plate. They are really tasty and anyone who loves chocolate will want seconds.

12 Oreo ® cookies
2 - 8 oz. packages cream cheese, softened
1/2 cup granulated sugar
1 tsp. vanilla
2 eggs, well beaten
1/2 cup semisweet chocolate chips

Preheat oven to 325F. Split cookies, keeping filling intact on one cookie half. Line twelve 2 1/2" muffin tins with foil baking cups. Place a filling-covered cookie half in each baking cup, filling side up. Set aside. In a large bowl beat cream cheese, sugar and vanilla until smooth. Add eggs all at once. Beat on low speed just till combined. Spoon filling into baking cups. Crush remaining cookies and sprinkle a little crushed cookie over filling in each cup. Use remaining crushed cookies as ice cream topping. Bake for 20 to 25 minutes or till set. Cool 1 hour. Cover and chill. Melt chocolate chips in microwave and drizzle onto plates and over baked cheesecake. Garnish with fresh strawberries.

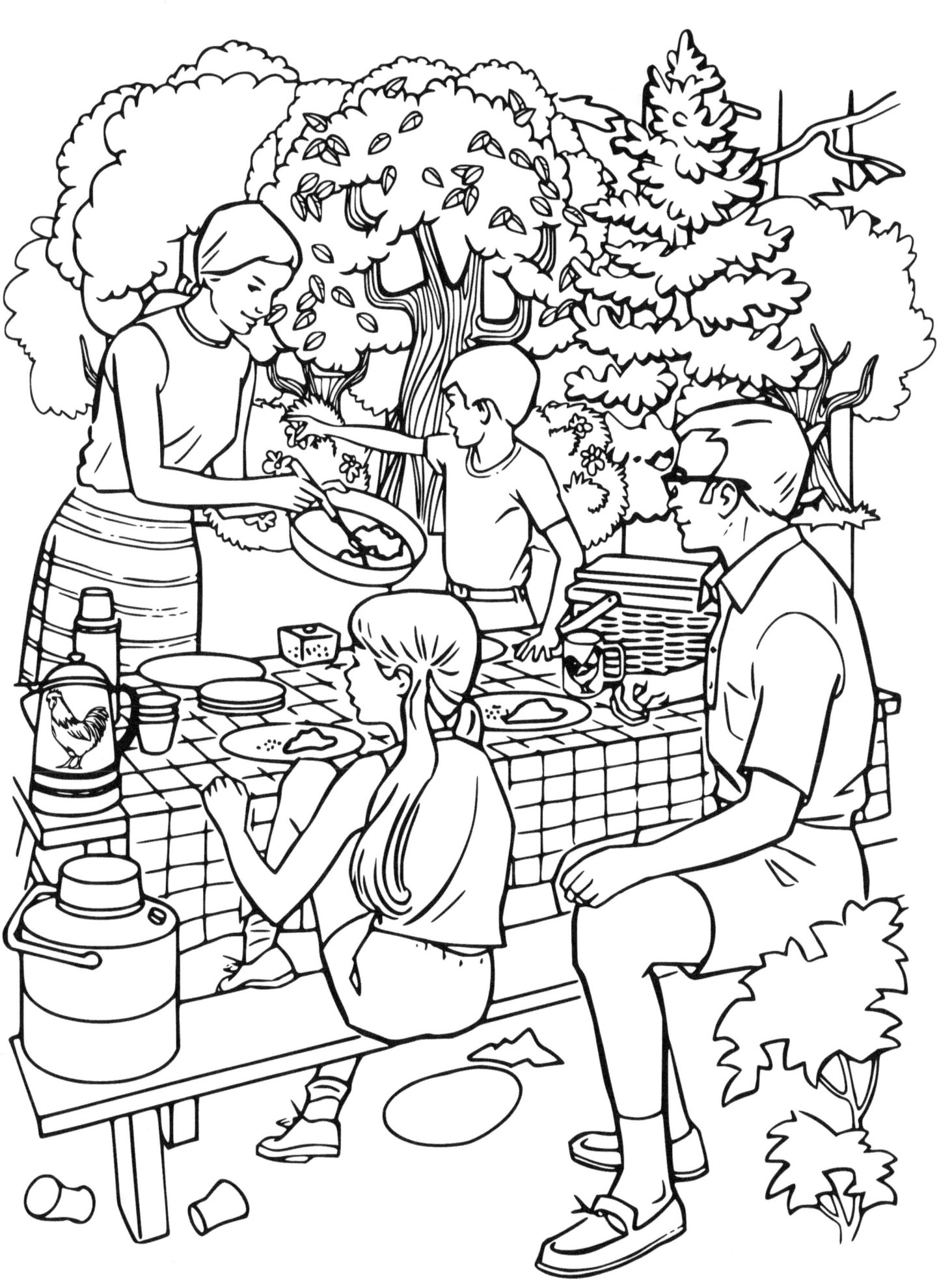

Brown Sugar Baked Beans

One of the things we enjoy when we go camping is a hot cup of coffee and toast made over the fire. We also like these beans. I make them ahead at home and bring them along. Then we just heat them in a pot and with toast over the fire and coffee they're wonderful.

3 - 14 oz. cans pork and beans
8 slices bacon, diced
3/4 cup brown sugar
1 tsp. dry mustard
1 medium onion, diced
1 - 2 garlic cloves, minced
1 1/2 tsp. basil
1 tsp. salt
1/4 tsp. pepper
2 tbsp. Worcestershire sauce

Preheat oven to 325F. Combine all ingredients in a 3 quart bean crock or large covered pot. Cover and bake for 2 1/2 hours, stirring occasionally. If beans start to dry out add a bit of water and 1/4 cup keetchup.

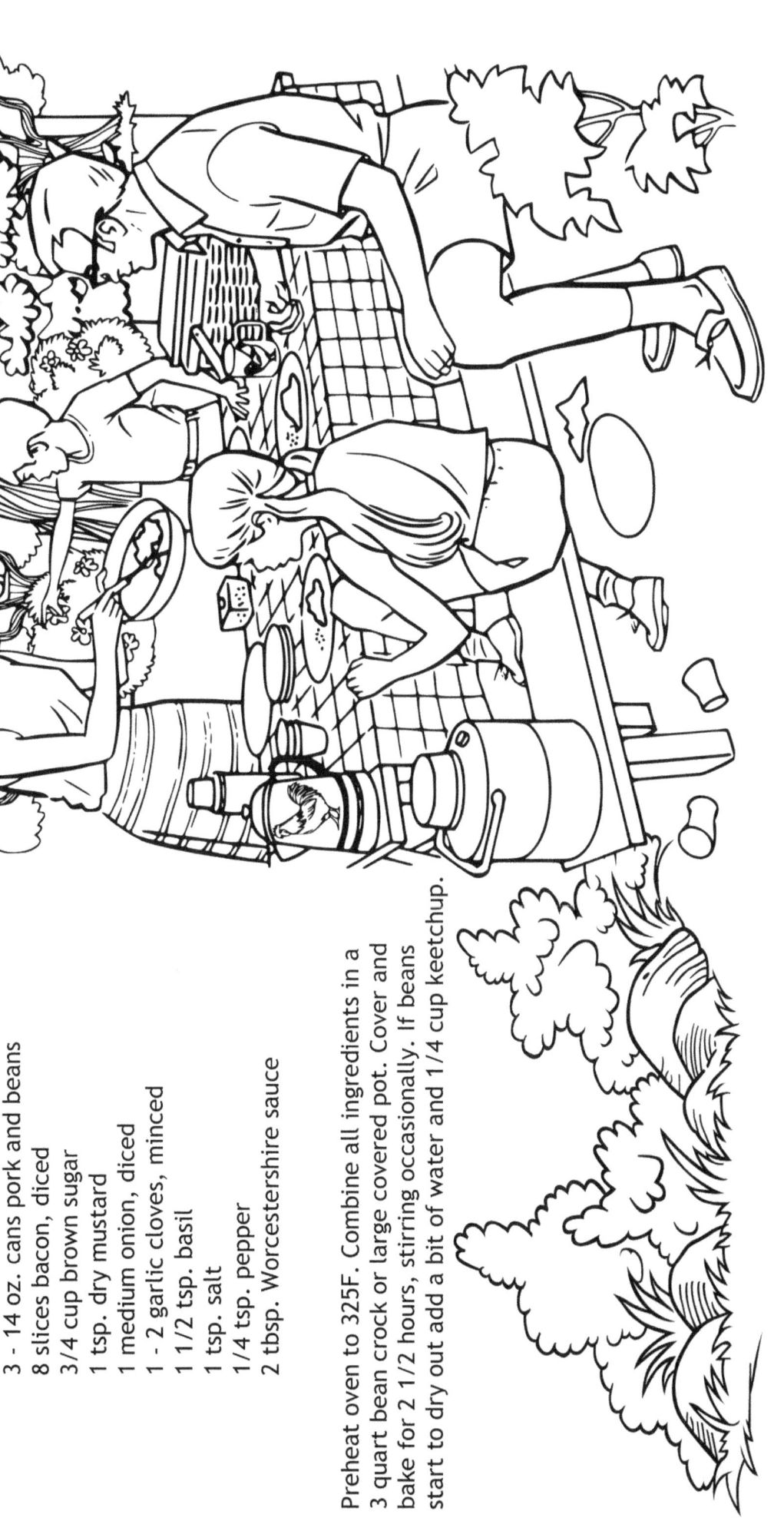

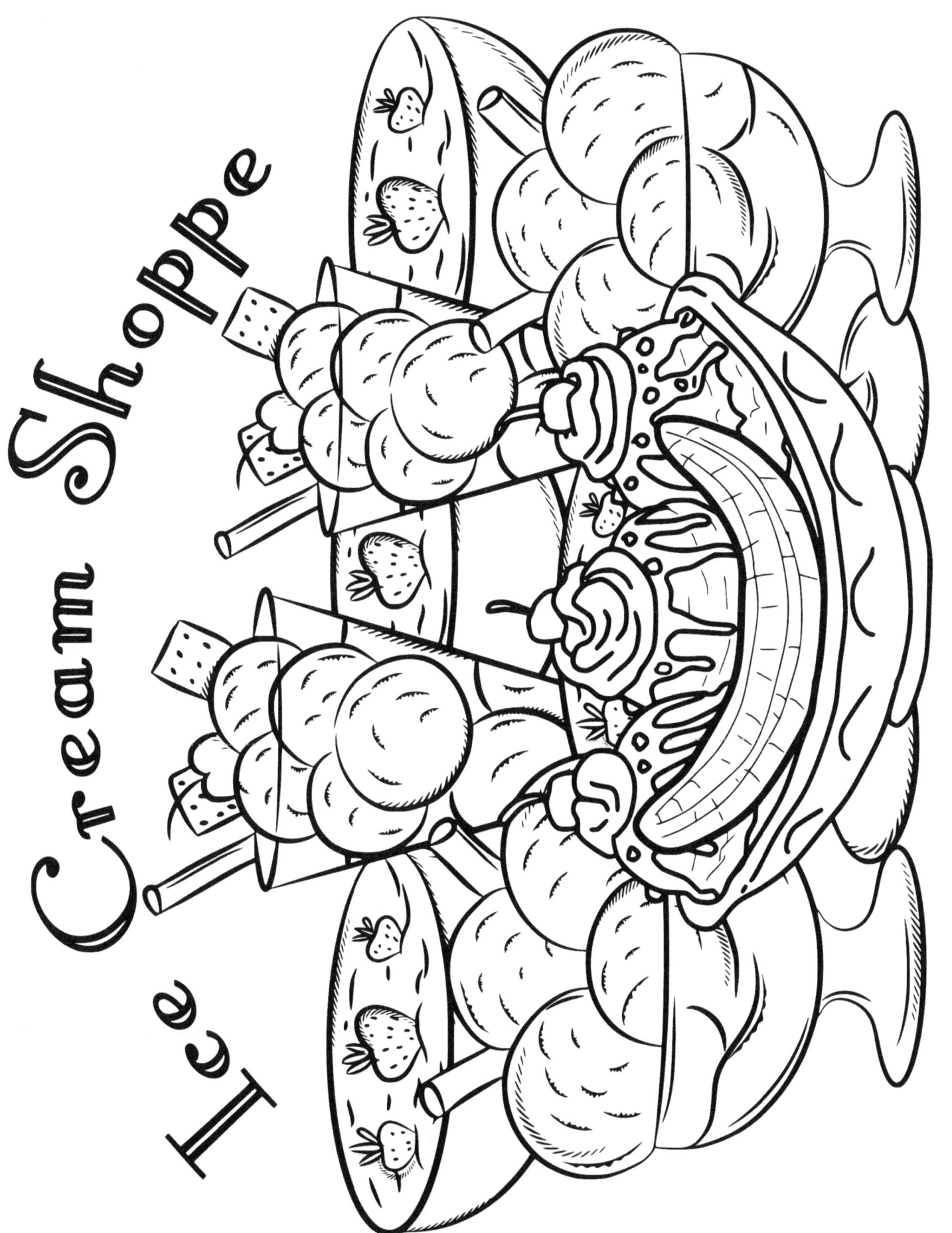

Ice Cream Shoppe

Blueberry Drops

When I was writing my cookie cookbook i created this recipe. Our family liked it so much I have made it often since then. If you're serving tea, make these cookies fairly small so they look more elegant. Otherwise, drop by teaspoonfuls as directed. These are really tasty served with icecream.

3/4 cup butter
2 eggs, beaten
2 tsp. baking powder
1/2 cup milk
1 1/2 cups fresh blueberries
1 tsp. cinnamon

3/4 cup granulated sugar
1 tsp. vanilla
1/2 tsp. salt
1 3/4 cups all-purpose flour
3 tbsp. brown sugar

Preheat oven to 350F. In a large bowl cream butter and sugar. Add eggs and beat thoroughly. Stir in vanilla, baking powder and salt. Alternately mix in milk and flour. Beat until smooth. Fold in blueberries. Drop by teaspoonfuls on ungreased cookie sheets. Combine cinnamon and sugar to make topping. Sprinkle over cookies. Bake for 12 - 15 minutes or until golden brown.

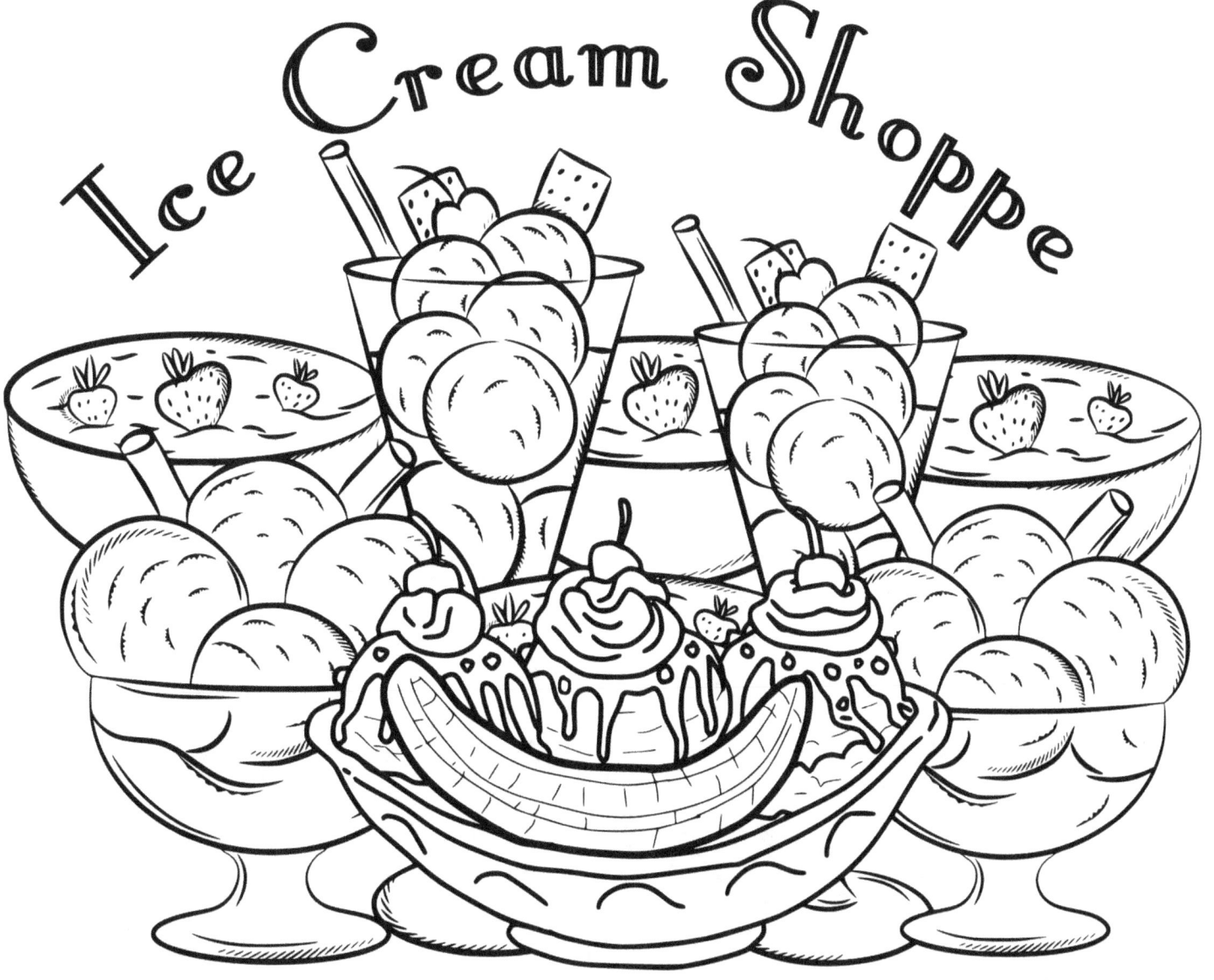

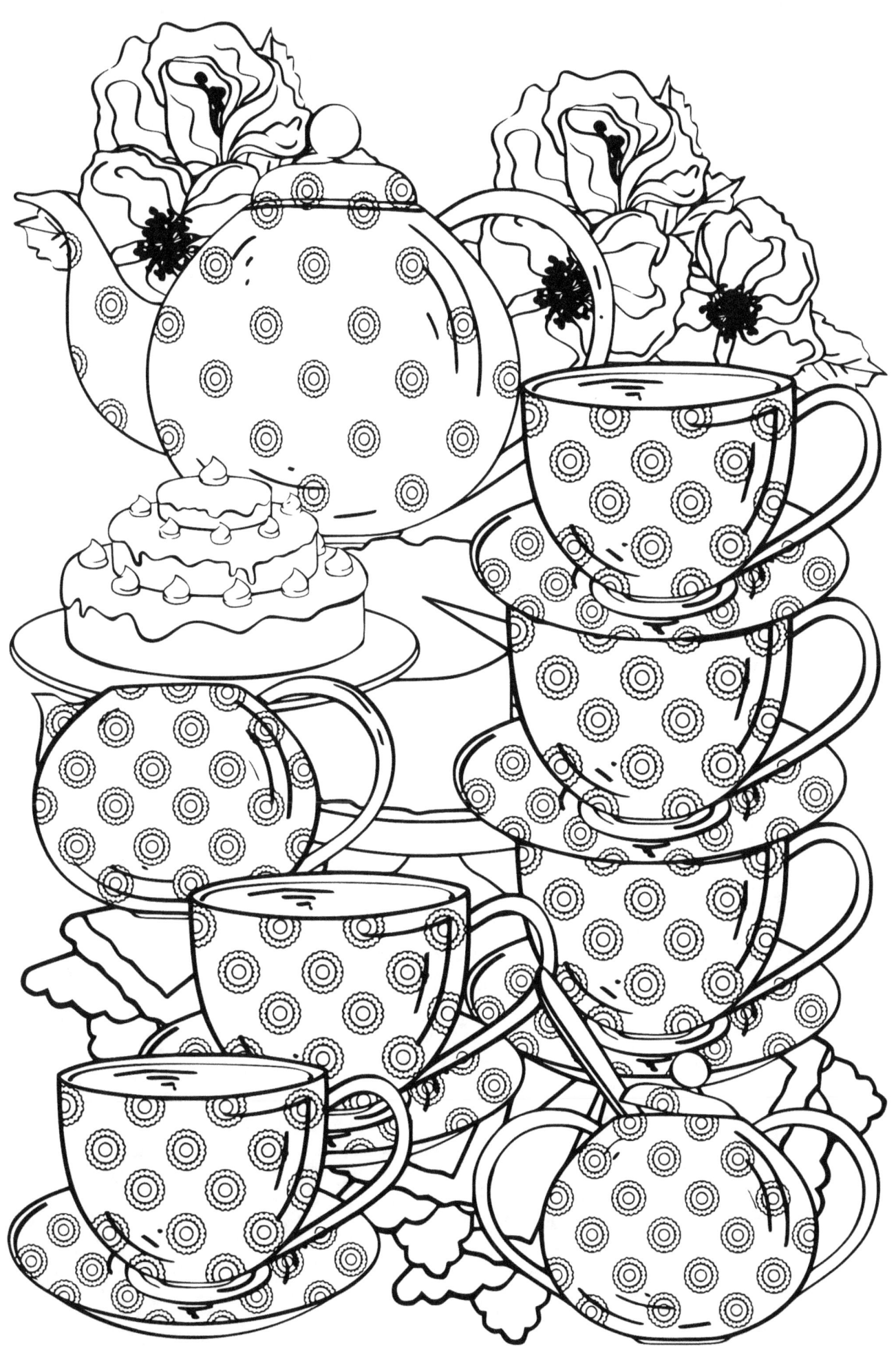

Lemon Loaf

I have been making this loaf for years and it's always moist and bursting with flavor. It never fails and is wonderful served with tea or coffee.

1/2 cup butter or margarine
2 eggs
1 1/2 cups all-purpose flour
1/2 tsp. salt

1 cup granulated sugar
1/2 cup milk
1 tsp. baking powder
Grated rind of one lemon

Glaze:
Juice of 1 lemon

1/4 cup granulated sugar

Preheat oven to 350F. In a large bowl cream butter and sugar. Add eggs and beat well. Blend in milk. In a second bowl mix flour, baking powder and salt. Fold in lemon rind. Pour over butter batter. Stir to moisten. Spoon into greased 9" x 5" bread pan. Bake for 1 hour or until a toothpick inserted in the center of the loaf comes out clean. Cool on rack for 10 minutes. Remove from pan. While loaf is still warm, combine juice and granulated sugar. Heat to dissolve sugar. Spoon evenly over top of loaf.

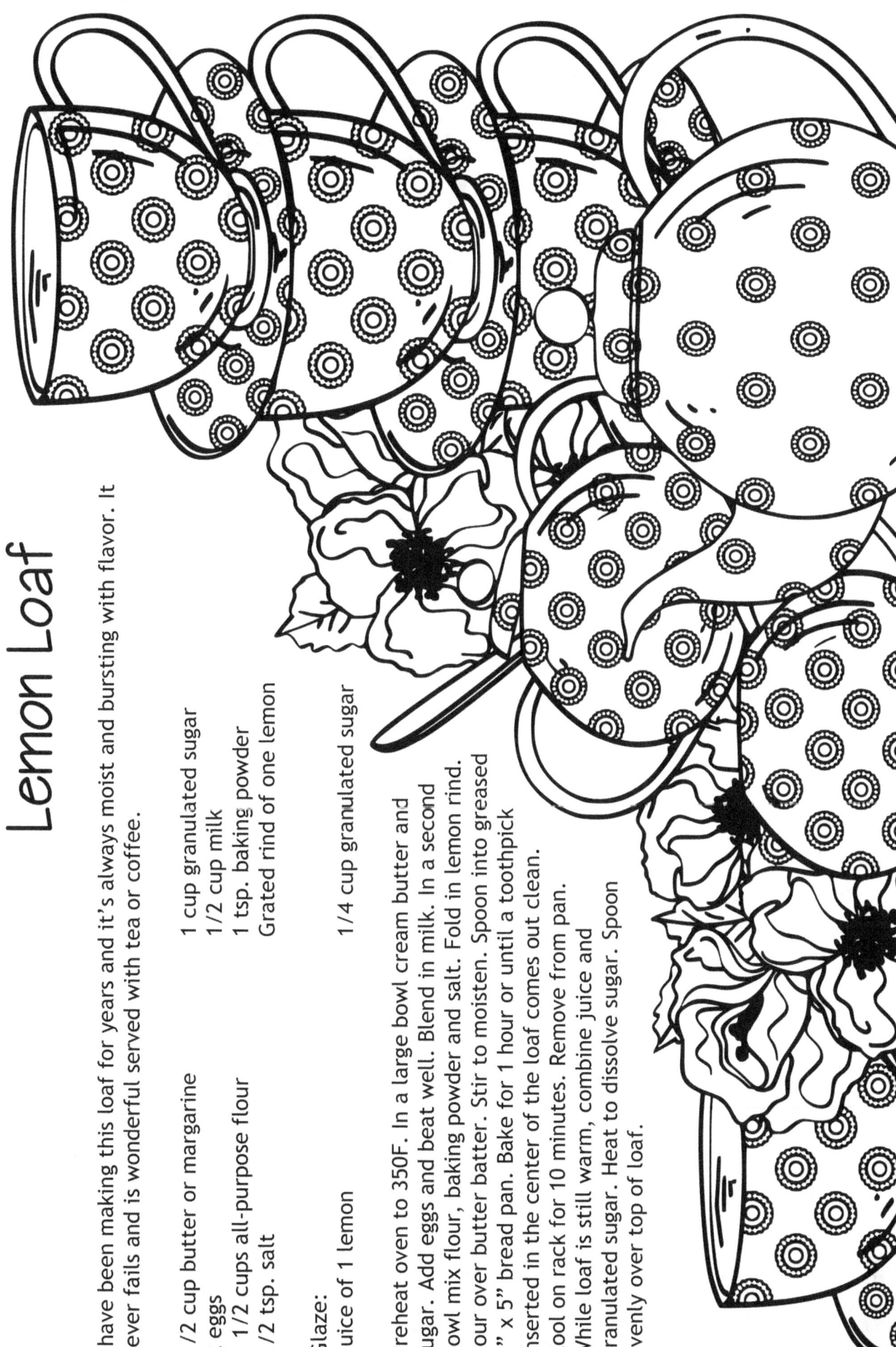

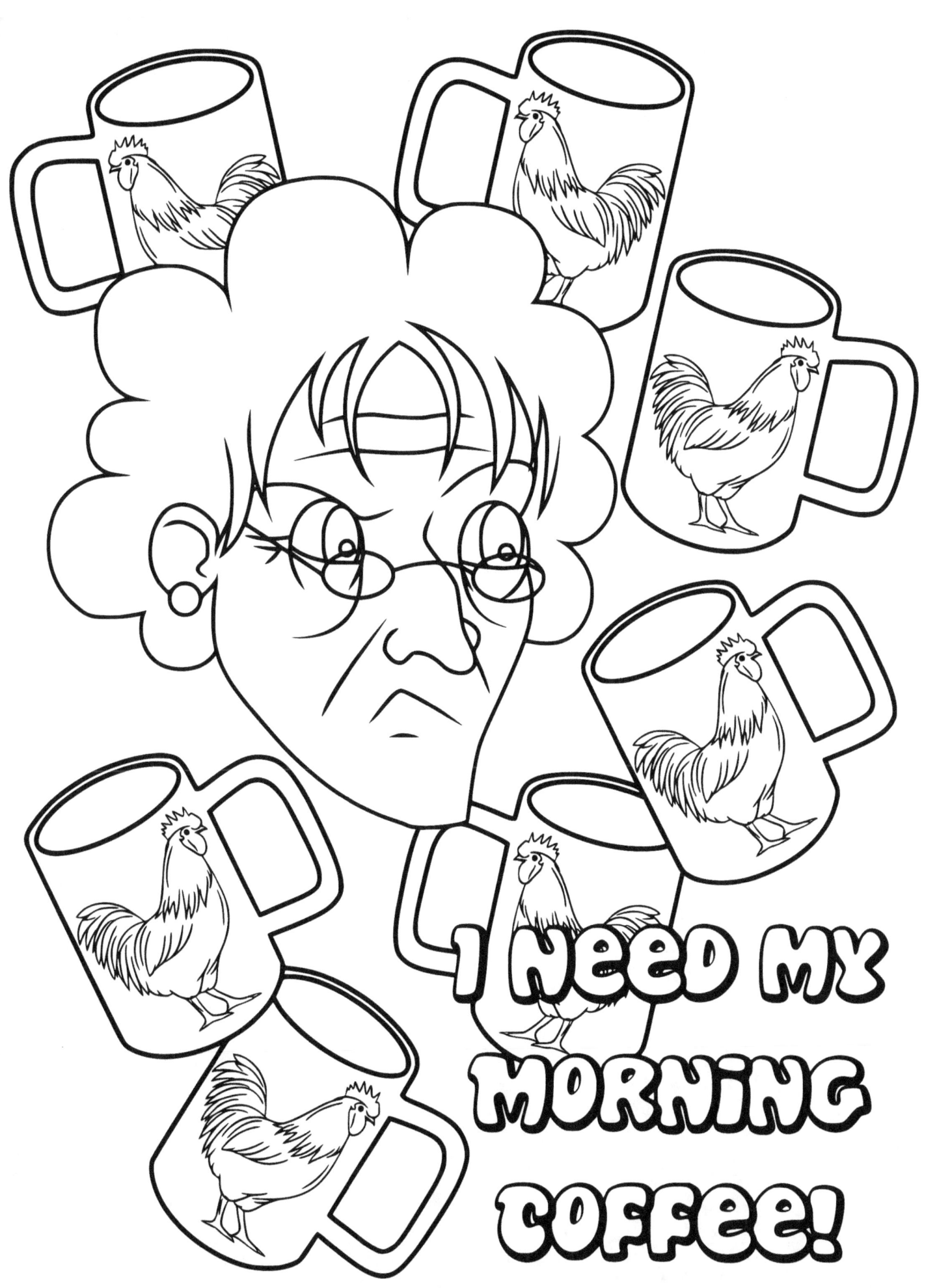

Peaches & Cream French Toast

With a strong cup of coffee this makes a perfect breakfast. It's great for those who have started the day off on the wrong foot too! Easy to make and simply delicious you'll love it and so will your family.

Peach Butter

1/3 cup peach jam   1/4 cup softened butter

French Toast

3 eggs   3 tbsp. peach jam
1/4 cup half-and-half   6 slices French bread
4 tbsp. butter

Topping

2 peaches, peeled, pitted and sliced
Maple syrup

For the peach butter, mix the jam and softened butter together. Beat until fluffy. Set aside.

For the French toast: Whisk together the eggs and second quantity of peach jam in a medium sized bowl. Beat in the half-and-half. Pour into a shallow pan to coat bread. Melt 2 tbsp. butter in a large frying pan. Dip both sides of bread in French toast mixture. Place in heated frying pan and allow to brown, about 4 to 5 minutes. Turn over and cook the second side. Repeat with the remaining bread slices. Serve with the peach butter and peaches and maple syrup.

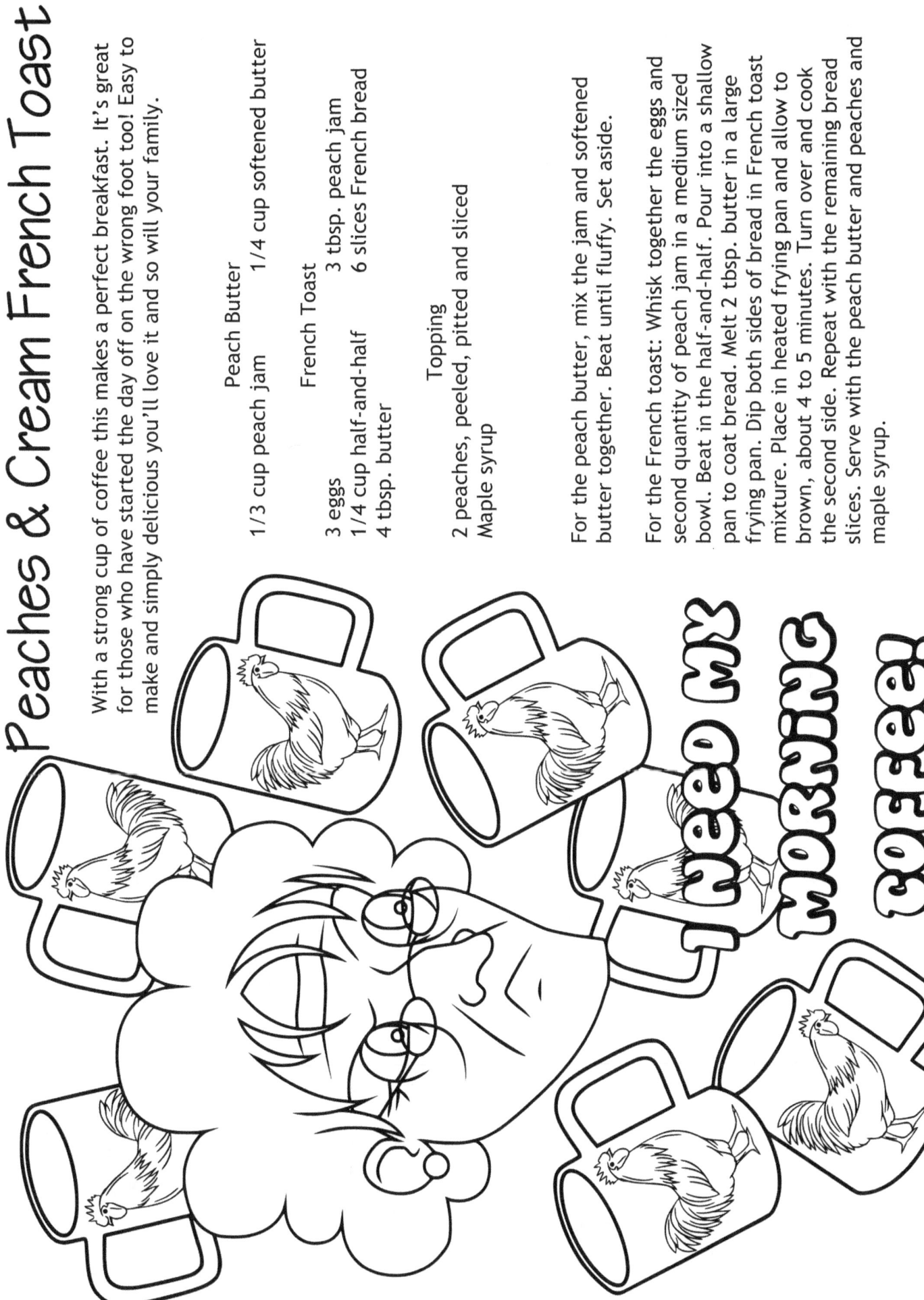

I NEED MY MORNING COFFEE!

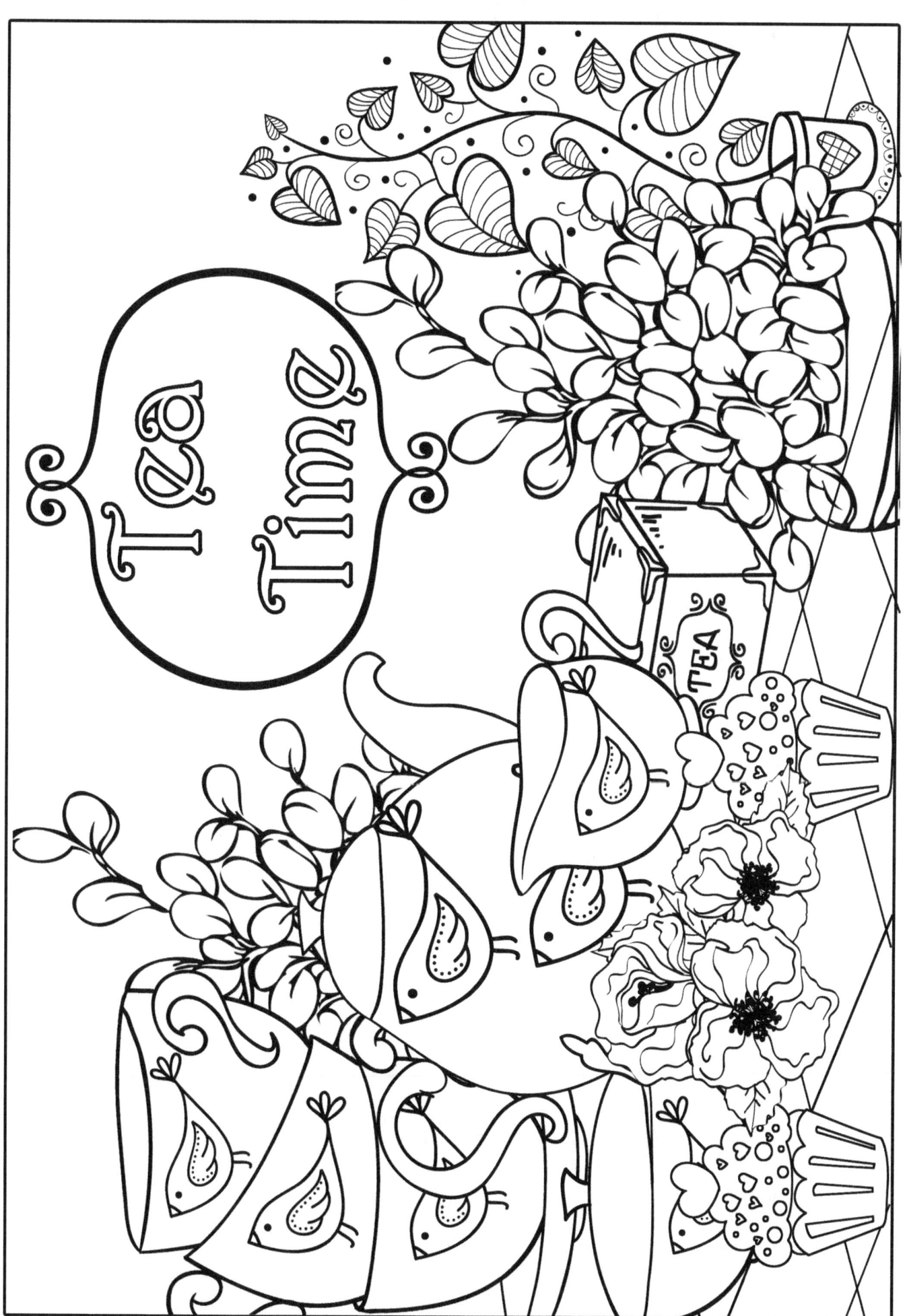

Pineapple Bread

This is another of those loaves that are always good. With the tangy taste of pineapple combined with the sweet taste of sugar this is a real treat. Moist and deliciopus every time you make it.

2 eggs
1 cup granulated sugar
1 tsp. vanilla
3 tsp. baking powder
3/4 tsp. salt

1/2 cup melted butter
1 cup crushed pineapple with juice
2 1/2 cups all-purpose flour
1/2 tsp. baking soda
1/2 cup chopped pecans (optional)

Preheat oven to 350F. In a mixing bowl beat eggs slightly. Add butter and sugar. Beat until smooth. Stir in pineapple and vanilla. In a separate bowl mix dry ingredients. Pour into pineapple mixture. Stir to moisten. Pour into greased 9" x 5" bread pan. Bake about 1 hour or until a toothpick inserted in the middle of the loaf comes out clean. Cool on a rack for 10 minutes. Remove from pan and continue to cool.

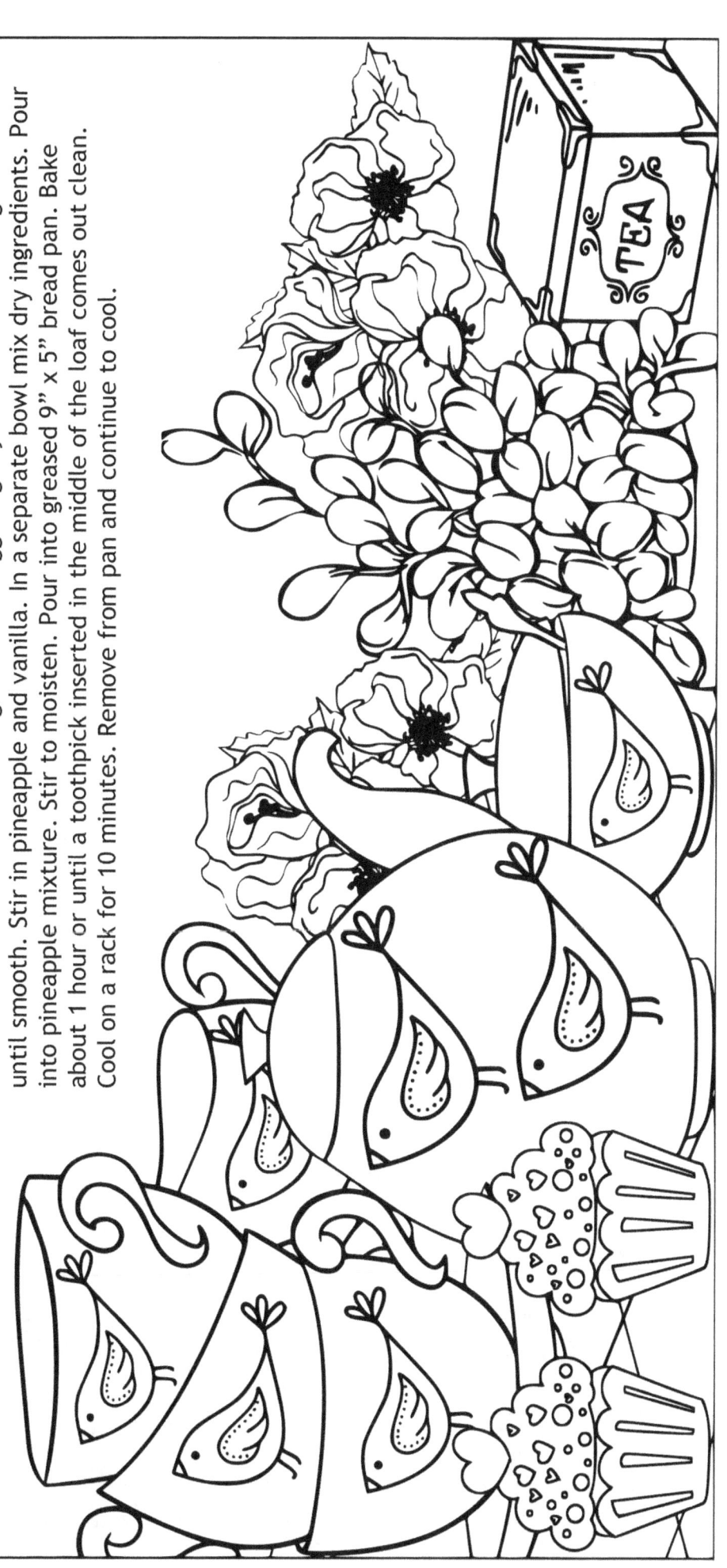

TEA

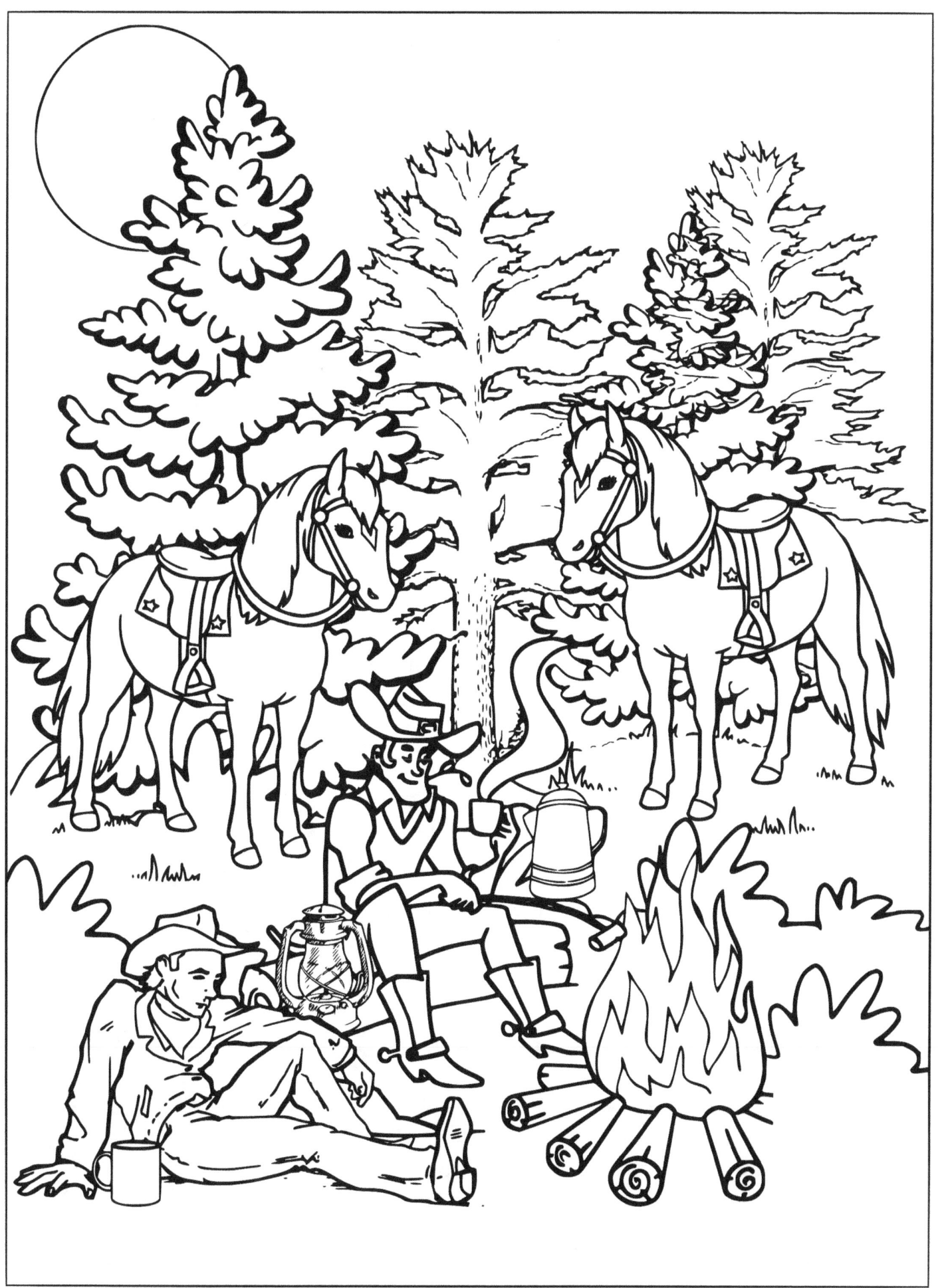

Corned Beef Hash

When cowboys are out on the range and come back to camp at night, they are tired, thirsty and hungry. They want a strong cup of coffee and lots of filling food. Corned beef hash fills the bill. I grew up on corned beef hash and still love it today. It's so easy and quick to make and it's one of our favorite dishes, like the cowboys.

1 medium onion, finely chopped
2 tbsp. bacon drippings or butter
6 cups cooked potatoes, cubed
12 oz. can corned beef, flaked
1 tsp. salt
1/2 tsp. pepper

In a large frying pan fry onions in bacon drippings until they are glossy (about 7 minutes). Add cubed potatoes, corned beef and salt and pepper. Stir well. We like our hash with some browned parts so I turn the burner up to about medium-high and let some of the bottom get a golden brown. Turn and repeat with other side. If you prefer not to have any crispy parts to your hash then keep the heat down around medium-low and stir the hash frequently until the hash is heated through.

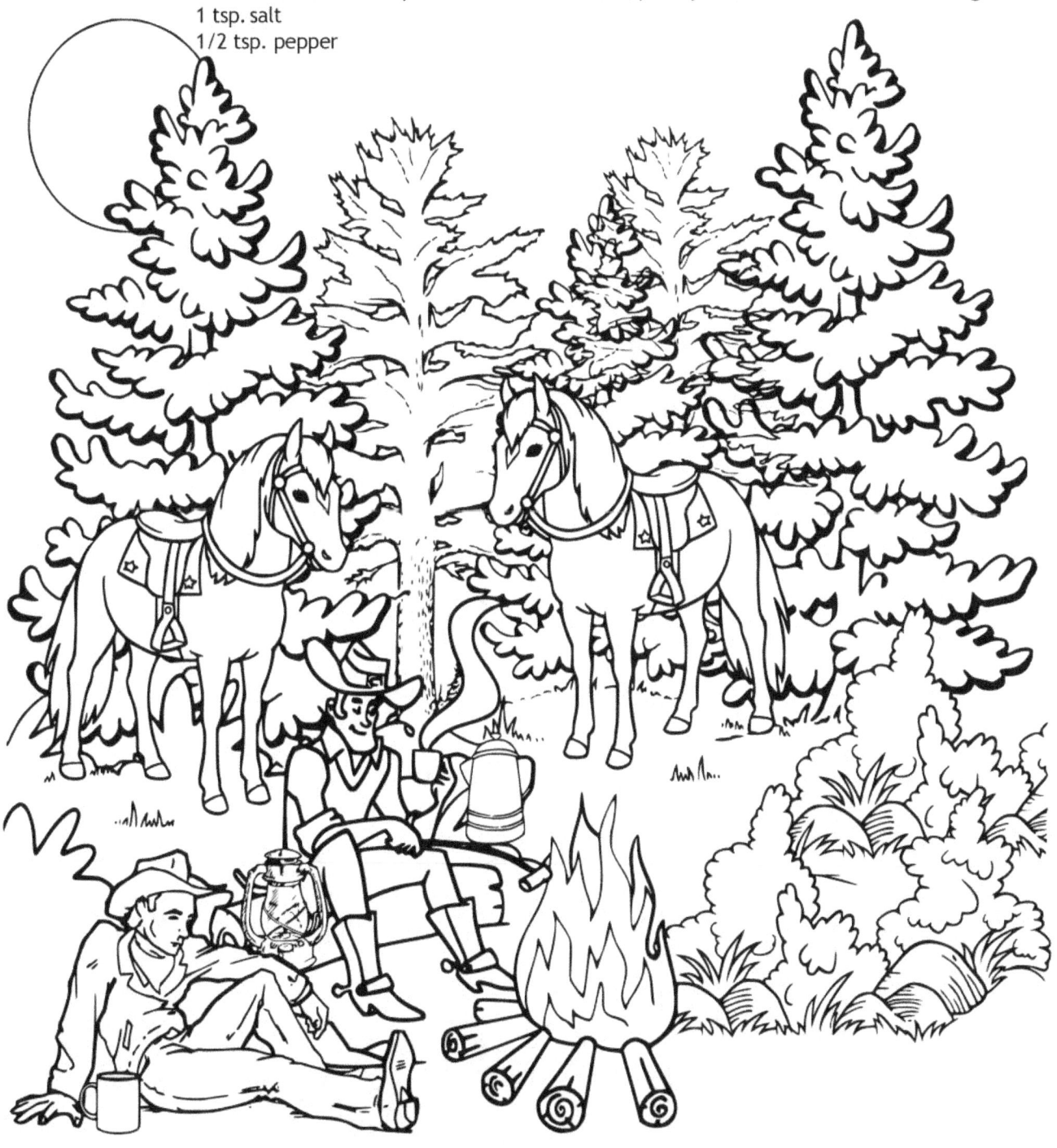

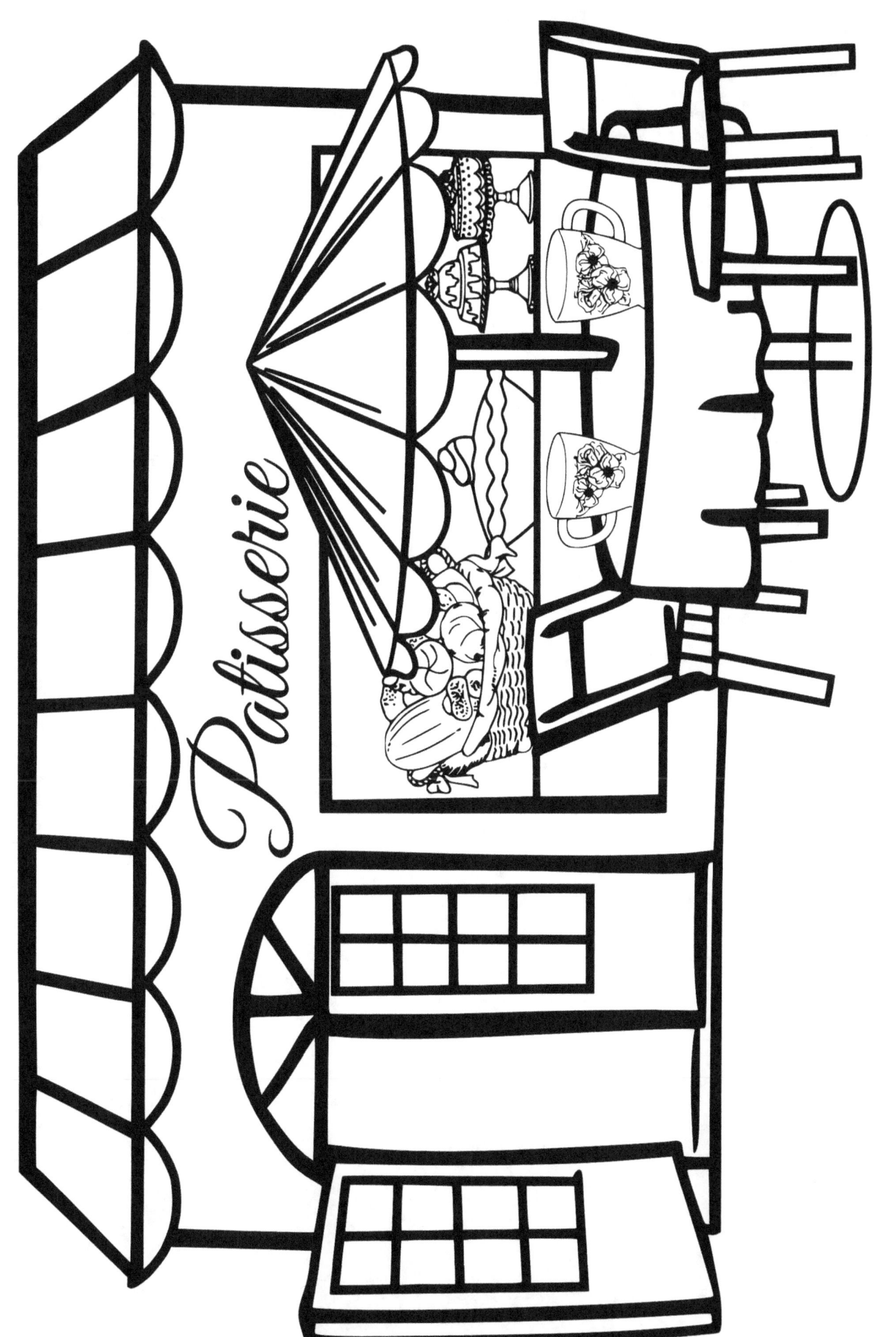

Cherry Ice Box Cookies

This is an easy cookie to make and handy to have in the freezer if unexpected company arrives. A pretty cookie, as the cherries give it a pale pink color.

1 cup butter or margarine (butter is better)
2 eggs
1/2 tsp. vanilla
1 tsp. salt
1 cup finely chopped cherries

1 cup granulated sugar
1 tsp. almond extract
2 tsp. baking powder
2 3/4 cups all-purpose flour

In a large bowl, cream butter and sugar together. Add eggs and beat thoroughly. Stir in almond extract, vanilla, baking powder and salt. Gradually mix in flour. Fold in cherries. Divide dough in half. Form each half into a long roll. Wrap in plastic wrap and refrigerate for at least 1 hour. When ready to bake, preheat oven to 400F. Cut rolls into slices and place on ungreased cookie sheets. The thinner the slices, the crisper the cookies and the less time needed to bake. For 1/4" thick slices, bake 8 - 10 minutes. For thicker slices bake a bit longer.

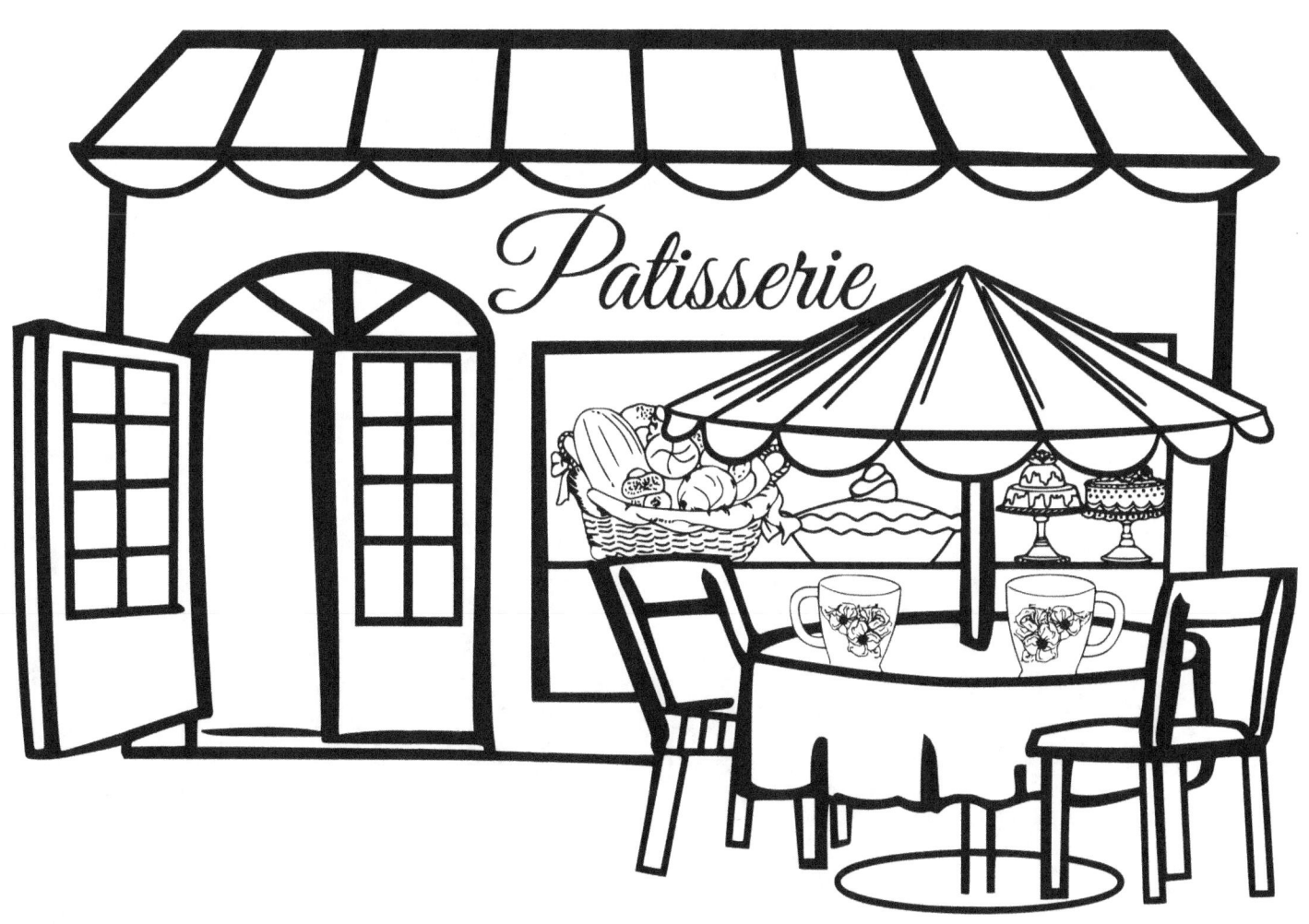

Thank You and Some Free Samples

At the moment I have several Easy Mandala books available so I am including samples from those books here so you can have an idea what they are like. On the following pages you will find samples from Easy Mandalas 1, Easy Mandalas 2 and Easy Mandalas 3. I will provide links to these books on Amazon as well. Hope you enjoy these free pages and that you will explore these other books.

And I want to thank you for purchasing my coloring book. I hope you have had many happy hours coloring the pictures in it. I am currently working on additional coloring books that you might enjoy.

If you'd like me to notify you when I have new books coming out or if you'd like to receive free pages occasionally, you can do so by joining my newsletter. Just go to www.coloringfunforadults.com/subscribe to join.

And please come visit my website and get some free coloring pages as well as coloring tips and more. To access my website, just go to www.coloringfunforadults.com

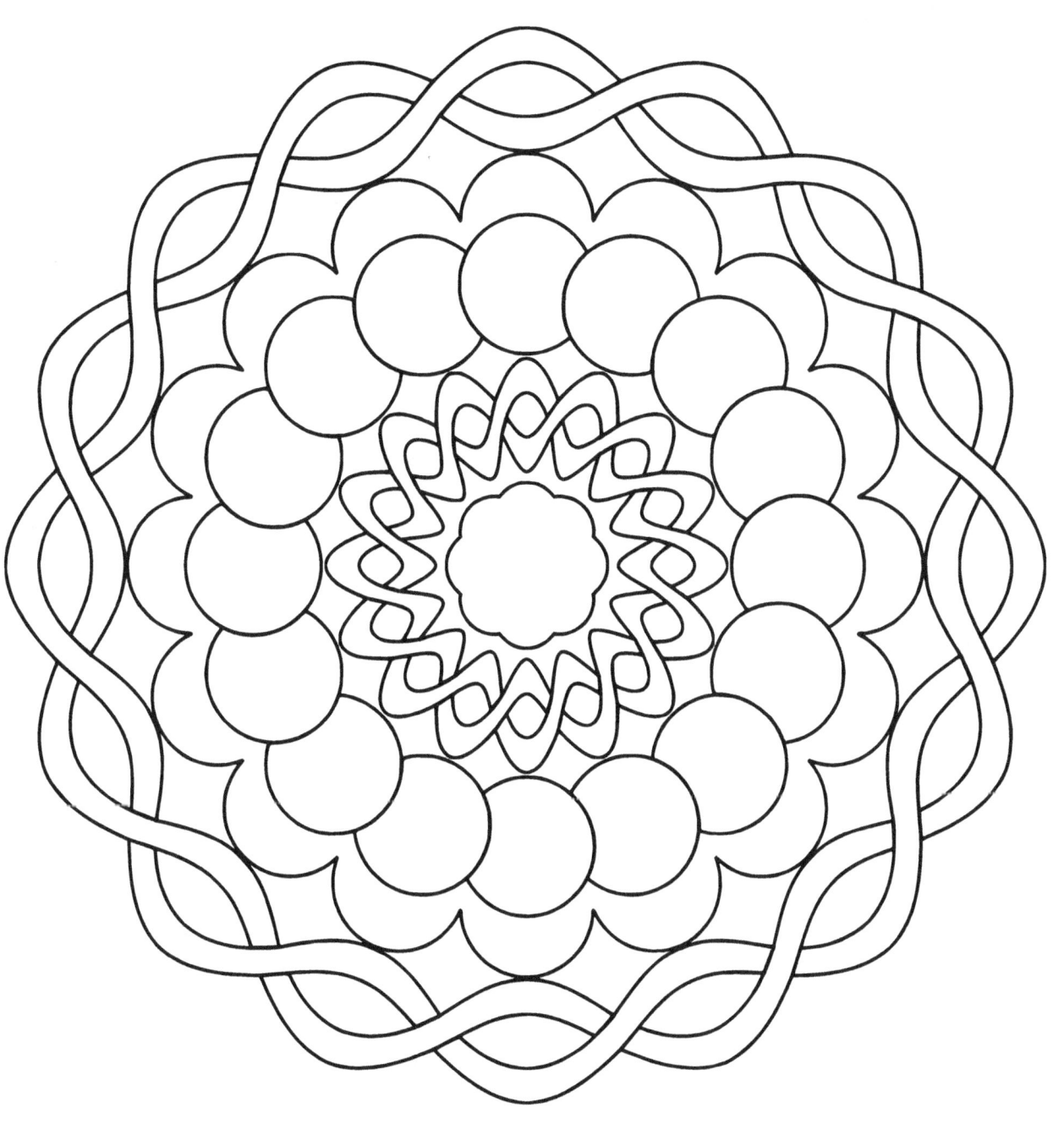

From Easy Mandalas 1: Adult Coloring Book. Go to www.amazon.com/dp/0973435720 to check it out.

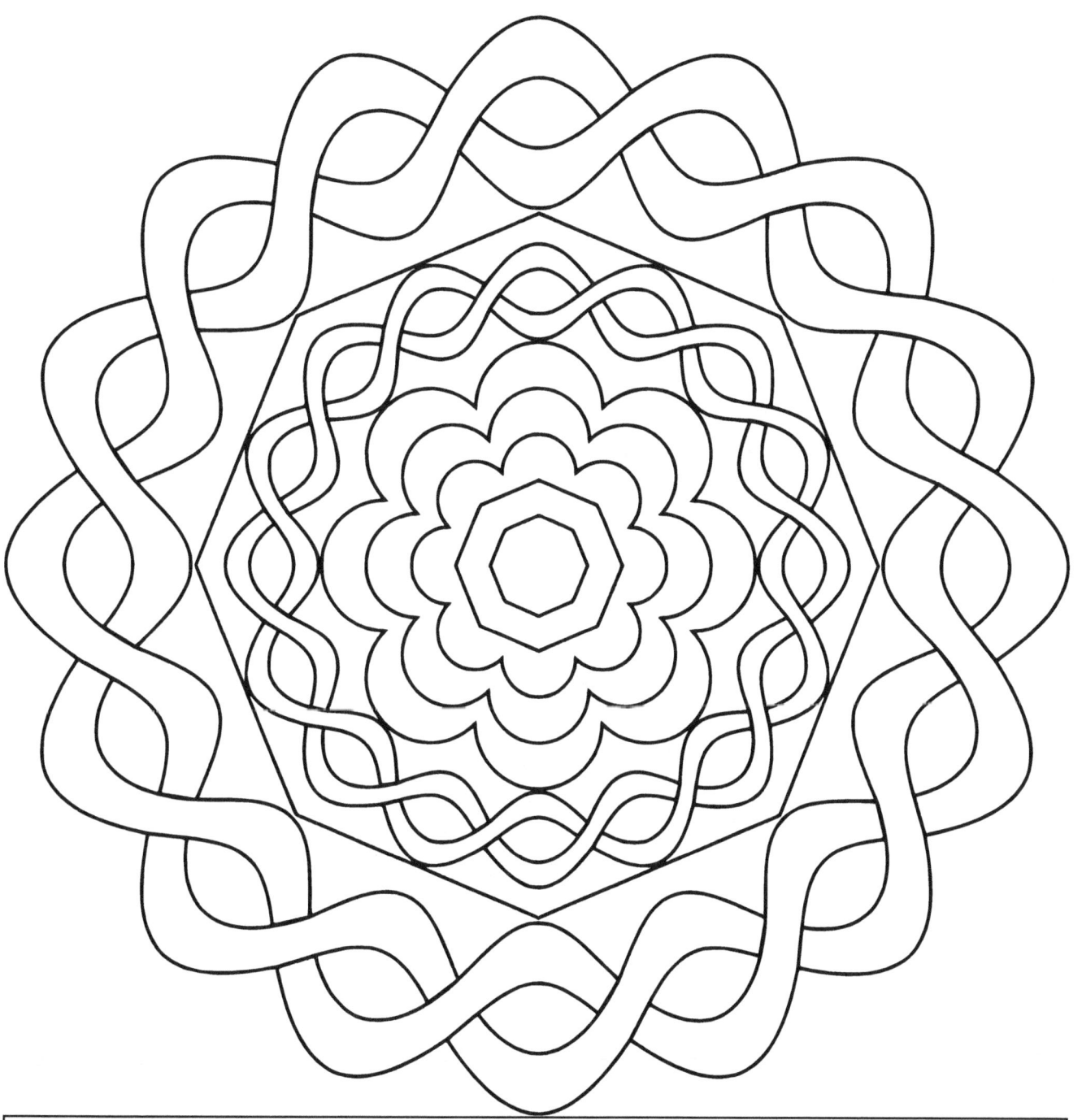

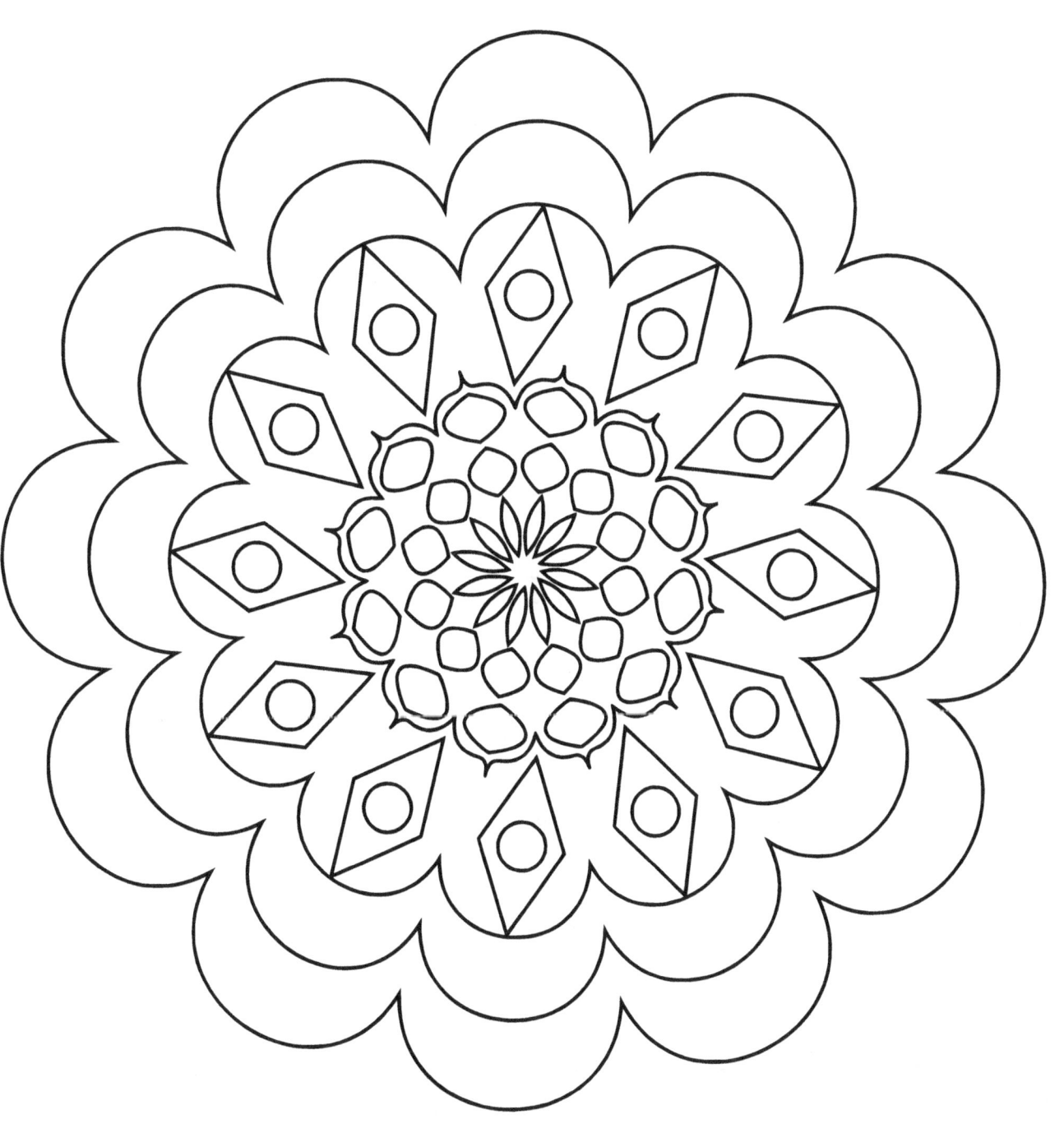

From Easy Mandalas 3: Adult Coloring Book. Go to www.amazon.com/dp/0973435771 to check it out.